CHRISTIANITY
stands
TRUE

A Common Sense
Look at the Evidence

CHRISTIANITY
stands
TRUE

A Common Sense
Look at the Evidence

LYNN GARDNER

COLLEGE PRESS
PUBLISHING COMPANY
Joplin, Missouri

Unless otherwise noted,
all Scripture quotations are taken from the
Revised Standard Version of the Bible,
copyrighted 1946, 1952, 1971
by the Division of Christian Education,
National Council of Churches of Christ of America.

Library of Congress Catalog Card Number # 93-74577
International Standard Book Number # 0-89900-677-9

This book is dedicated to the three children
God has given to Barbara and me:

Bryce Kevin Gardner
Mark Todd Gardner
Kara Dawn Arnce

"Behold, children are a gift of the Lord."
(Psalm 127:3, NASB)

ACKNOWLEDGMENTS

Over the last several years I have made over 200 presentations of a slide-illustrated series of talks on the theme "Christianity Stands True." The material in these presentations has been expanded and developed into this book.

I am indebted to Seth Wilson, long-time dean and professor at Ozark Christian College, who convinced me of the need for popular-level teaching on Christian evidences in churches. He emphasized, "Don't go out and demand that people believe. Give them reasons for faith." Ralph Mehrens provided the technical expertise in producing slides for the series.

I am most grateful to my wife, Barbara, and our three children — Bryce, Mark, and Kara — for helping in many ways in developing the material. They have heard my series dozens of times. In fact, my sons, when they were ten and twelve, told me that if I suddenly became ill they could take over and give the talks for me.

It has been a blessing in my life to teach in the area of evidences and apologetics in Bible college for 28 years.

I express appreciation to College Press Publishing Company for making this book a reality. Credit is given to Paula Nash Giltner for the pictures of biblical persons that appear in this book. Credit is given to Michael Lawson for the picture of the ants and aphids.

Good News Productions, International of Joplin, Missouri, is developing audio-visual materials based on the content of this book.

CONTENTS

FOREWORD

In today's world, the value of Christian Evidences is under attack from two opposite directions. For the most part the secular world simply ignores the claims of Christianity. The assumption prevails that Christianity, like all other religions, is a relic from the unenlightened past that hangs on particularly among the uneducated, who are unable or unwilling to face the sober reality that there is no god, no individual human life beyond the grave and no ultimate purpose or meaning in the universe beyond what we create for ourselves. So-called "evidences" for faith are in reality nothing but rationalizations to buttress a wavering faith that cannot be supported rationally yet emotionally dare not be dropped. The most consistent secularists are quite willing to acknowledge that with the "death" of the God idea also dies any trust in our own nature as rational beings.

Nearly a century ago the secular educator, John Dewey, argued that all our truth is only our way of making adjustments to our environment; and we should not think we have arrived at any objective truth corresponding in any meaningful way to what really is. The irony of his position is that he and those who agree with him today continue to write books and have the gall to lecture the rest of us about why we ought to give up our antiquated views of what constitutes truth and how it can be arrived at.

Unfortunately in what Christians believe to be a counsel of despair, many have denied the value of evidence to support religious or Christian faith. This attack against evidence comes from those who would reduce religion (and in some cases Christianity) to a matter of feeling or, perhaps, even love with no concern about the need for truth and, therefore

11

also, no concern about any need for evidences to support the truth. Even some who, as Christians, are clearly committed to its objective truth claims, sometimes reject the validity and value of Christian evidence. In a sense, Christianity is reduced to a marvelous idea which can never be substantiated by evidence or an appeal to reason but is so good and helpful that we must believe it to be true.

The Biblically grounded Christian is preserved from both of these extremes. Across the millennia, however, Christian thinkers have taught with great consistency that human reason and the use of evidences have an important though carefully limited role in Christian experience and ministry. They argued, in fact, that man was created like God (Genesis 1:2 and Genesis 5:3); and this image of God included both a rational faculty (Colossians 3:10) and a capacity for fellowship with God (Ephesians 4:24). Man thus possesses naturally an innate knowledge of God and His law (Romans 2:14,15; Romans 1:19-21), not in the sense of a set of propositions within the mind at birth, but of an inner adaptability to and fitness for the knowledge of God (i.e., man's mind is no tabula rasa but is like a violin case which just fits the instrument it was prepared to receive).

The objective evidence for the existence of God, the supernaturalness of Christianity, and the truth of Scripture is completely sufficient to lead to certainty (or to probability of a near infinite degree) for all honest unbiased minds (Romans 1:18-25; John 5:33-36; Acts 1:33; and a multitude of other passages). And these evidences are to be preached in our witness to unbelievers (see Isaiah 1:18; Deuteronomy 13 and 18; and 2 Peter 3:15).

Unfortunately the minds of no man since the fall of Adam are honest and unbiased. Sin has corrupted the innate knowledge of God and has vitiated the ability of man to evaluate properly the objective evidence (1 Corinthians 1:14 and Romans chapters 1-3).

This corruption of the intellect, however, is not total. The degree to which it is destructive depends upon the closeness of the objects of knowledge to the things that are truly vital to

Christianity. In the field of mathematics, for example, the natural man reasons for all practical purposes as well as the saved man (Luke 15:8). The knowledge of the existence and nature of God is tremendously more vital to the development of our spiritual life; and hence, sin vitiates the mind to a much greater degree when it attends to this object. The resurrection of Jesus, His deity, and the atonement still more vitally affect the spiritual life; hence at this point man's mind is most darkened by sin (cf. again Romans 2:20,21 and 1 Corinthians 2:14).

Despite the effects of sin, however, the natural man often arrives at a somewhat erroneous idea of God, may know that He exists and has an eternal and infinite nature (Romans 1:20,21 and James 2:19), may know that He is to be worshiped (Acts 17:23), may know the moral law of right and wrong (Romans 2:14,15) and on some few occasions may actually know the way of salvation (Hebrews 6:4 and 2 Peter 2:21). All this is by common grace.

The ultimate unproved assumption of apologetics is that there is such a thing as truth. By truth, we mean meaningful correspondence to the standard of actuality. We have a right to assume this, because it cannot be denied (cf. Augustine — to deny it is in actuality not only to affirm truth but to claim that one has it). And we test truth by showing that it is systematically coherent. It is horizontally consistent within itself and vertically fits the facts of the external world.

Truth is not something above God to which He must be brought to judgment. Truth is an aspect of God's nature — an attribute of God. True, God always chooses to do what is in conformity with His own nature. He is always consistent with Himself because it is His eternal nature to be so.

We could begin our apologetic with God as our postulated hypothesis. If we did, we would discover, if we thought correctly, that we really would have no right to trust our reason except for the fact that God is a rational God and created us like Himself and a rational world that conforms to (is amenable to) His thought and ours.

On the other hand, if we begin with truth, we shall, if we

think rightly, discover that this leads us to the conclusion that God is and the Bible is His revelation of Himself to us. This is where Lynn Gardner begins in his fine book, *Christianity Stands True: A Common Sense Look at the Evidence*. It represents a scripturally approved and, indeed, a divinely commanded way to carry on our witness for Christ. Unless an unbeliever's mind has been corroded by a false philosophy, he is willing to agree that there is such a thing as truth and that it is worth pursuing.

Then, step by step, in an easily intelligible style that is both interesting and convincing, Lynn Gardner shows that many common ideas about religion and about Christianity simply do not fit the facts of the universe in which we live. If he seeks to be consistent, the non-Christian must either give up these non-Christian views or accept the truth of Christianity.

Unfortunately in our day, the church has not done an effective job of presenting unbelievers with a consistent, intelligible and interesting case for Christianity. It has not even done so to its own membership. Worst of all, it has not presented such a case to its own children. We are thus raising a generation of untaught church members — Christians, but so ill-informed they are totally unable to carry on an intelligent discussion with an unbeliever about our faith.

We can show by our life that Christian faith is worthwhile. Many unbelievers are won by it. But even more are turned off because they think Christian faith is only a delightful fantasy. It would be wonderful if there were a god who loves us and cares for us as Christianity claims, but such wishful thinking does not square with the harsh realities of the real world.

Lynn Gardner seeks to meet this challenge head-on. In simple convincing style he presents the claims of the gospel and calls the unbeliever to rethink his unexamined philosophy of life. He challenges the non-Christian to consider the facts of life and square them honestly with what he believes. He challenges the non-Christian to be consistent and to turn to a valid understanding of God, the world and man — in short to a Christian world-and-life view that is internally consistent and fits the realities of the universe about us.

FOREWORD

In presenting this material Lynn Gardner does a remarkable job of explaining even complex problems with clarity, humor and apt illustrations that add up to a fascinating and convincing case for the truth of Christianity. Pastors, Sunday school teachers and lay persons who are concerned to meet the intellectual challenge of unbelievers will find this book invaluable. We need to be ready to give a reason for the hope within us to all those who deep down inside themselves know they need and, in fact, deeply long for the very message we Christians want to give them.

Kenneth S. Kantzer
Trinity Christian University

INTRODUCTION

A skeptic taunted a Christian, "Believers are touchy and offended when asked why they believe in Christianity because the awkward truth is that they have no reason, they just feel like believing."

We do have good evidence for believing that Christianity is true. Faith is not "believing what you know isn't so," as a child misunderstood. Faith is trust based on sufficient evidence.

Purpose and Summary

Christianity Stands True presents evidences that support the truth of Christianity. The purpose of this book is to give a common sense, non-technical presentation of evidences supporting the truth of Christianity. An honest seeker will learn the basis of the Christian faith. The Christian's confidence that Christianity is true will be strengthened.

The first six chapters state a case for Christianity based on evidence for the historical reliability of the New Testament records. Historically rooted, supernatural evidences support the claims of Jesus of Nazareth that He was God in flesh. Because He is deity we can accept Jesus' teaching that the Old Testament is the Word of God and that the New Testament is the Word of God in fulfillment of His promises to the apostles.

The last four chapters trace two confirming lines of evidence. Evidence of design in the physical universe, the human body and the plant and animal world point to a Divine Designer. Christianity rings true in life as it meets the needs of the human heart for meaning, freedom, peace, love and hope. *Christianity does in fact stand true.*

General Features

1. *Christianity Stands True* is a concise, popular-level statement of the evidences supporting the truth of Christianity. It is not intended to be comprehensive, detailed, nor technical. Basic issues have been handled but no effort has been made to cover all objections on each topic.

2. The book follows a logical pattern of argument. The direct line of evidence seeks to establish the reliability of the New Testament books, the deity of Jesus, and the inspiration of the Bible. The evidence of design in nature and experience in life are used as confirming lines of evidence. This common sense approach will appeal to the general reader.

3. The material in this book has been field-tested through communication with many audiences. Slide-illustrated talks presenting the content of this manuscript have been given in churches, colleges, and conventions. Effort has been made to choose headings, outlines, and illustrations that readily communicate.

Readers

The general reader can read this book easily because of the illustrations and non-technical language. As a tool in evangelism it can be given to help honest seekers investigate the basis of the Christian faith. It can be used in the local church and campus fellowship as a faith-building study. It could be used in a freshman evidences course in Bible college.

The primary audience would be thinking people—adults, including college and high school students—who are interested in Christianity but are not experts on theology. *Christianity Stands True* seeks to build basic faith in those seeking answers to life's basic questions and to strengthen the faith in believers.

"In as much as many have undertaken to compile a narrative of the things which have been accomplished among us, just as they were delivered to us by those who from the beginning were eyewitnesses and ministers of the word. It seemed good to me also, having followed all things closely from some time past, to write an orderly account for you most excellent Theophilus that you may know the truth concerning the things of which you have been informed."   *Luke 1:1-4*

"No better summary of the best elements of modern historical method can be found in the accepted modern manuals on historical method [than Luke's summary in Luke 1:1-4]."

Earle E. Cairns

"There is no body of ancient literature in the whole world which enjoys such a wealth of good textual attestation as the New Testament."   *F. F. Bruce*

Chapter One
THE NEW TESTAMENT STANDS TRUE AS HISTORY

PART 1 — AUTHORS AND TEXT

The New Testament is the primary source for our knowledge of Jesus Christ. The case for Christianity in this book does not begin by assuming the deity of Jesus or the inspiration of the Bible. The beginning point is an investigation of the evidence for the historical reliability of the New Testament records. How can we in the twentieth century come to know God? Has God directly communicated in any way with man on earth? The New Testament records help one answer these questions. The best starting point is a consideration of the reliability of the New Testament books because our knowledge of Christ depends on them. Christians claim that in the first century God actually came to earth in the person of Jesus of Nazareth. Does factual evidence support this claim? Some people challenge the Christian believer with comments and questions like these:

"Several people just wrote down legends about a man called Jesus!"

"The books have been copied so many times. How do you know they haven't been changed?"

"Religious books tell about emotional experiences. They have no basis in historical fact."

Some people today reject the New Testament as history because of their basic assumptions. Those who start by assuming miracles cannot happen, will reject the New Testament because it tells of miracles. Others say, "I'm not going to pin my faith on a book written 2,000 years ago. Truth is constantly changing. I want an up-to-date faith." Still others will say, "This book is unacceptable because it does not agree with my ideas and thinking."

This kind of thinking resembles that of a man who thought he was dead. His psychiatrist convinced him that dead men don't bleed. Then the doctor jabbed a needle into the man's finger. Blood spurted out. The man exclaimed, "Oh! Dead men do bleed after all!" He was not willing to change his beliefs to fit the facts so he reinterpreted the facts to fit his thinking.

A Christian philosophy teacher was speaking at a banquet. His wife was with him and she was conversing with a Hindu man at the table. She said, "The reason I believe Christianity is true is that it gives me peace in my heart." He responded, "You know that is just why I'm a Hindu. It gives me peace!"

What objective evidence can a Christian present to a non-Christian? Subjective evidence can be given to support any view. Evidence outside of one's own subjective experience also supports the truth of Christianity. We should give open and honest consideration to the objective evidence for the reliability of the New Testament and base our conclusion on those facts.

In investigating the reliability of any historical source these three questions need to be considered:

Who is the actual author?

Has the book been copied correctly since its time of writing?

Is the book a historically true account of what happened?

With an open mind we should ask these questions about the New Testament books, especially the Gospel accounts since they record the life of Jesus. Do the New Testament books meet the tests of good history?

Actual Authors?

Who were the actual authors of the New Testament books? Were they written by persons who knew the facts? By eye-witnesses? Any evidence of forgery? Does any known evidence prove that any claimed author could not have written the book? Do the books date from the lifetime of the claimed authors?

Some reject the claim of authors of the New Testament books. Sydney J. Harris, newspaper columnist, wrote, "Nobody who wrote the New Testament had come into actual contact with Jesus." He rejects what he calls "the historical fallacy that the Gospels spring from men who actually saw and heard what they report."[1] Harris stated that biblical scholars agreed with his conclusions, but gave no evidence from the primary sources.

The New Testament documents record the testimony of those who were eyewitnesses to Christ. Being a witness to Christ meant telling exactly what one had seen Him do and heard Him speak. When the apostles were threatened by Jewish authorities, they said, "We cannot but speak of what we have seen and heard" (Acts 4:20).

The authors of some New Testament books claim to be writing eyewitness accounts. Peter often claimed to be a witness of Jesus in his preaching (Acts 2:32; 3:15; 5:32; 10:39-42) and in his writings (1 Peter 5:1; 2 Peter 1:16-18). He wrote, "For we did not follow cleverly devised myths when we made known to you the power and coming of our Lord Jesus Christ, but we were eyewitnesses of His majesty" (2 Peter 1:16).

The author of the fourth Gospel said, "He who saw it has borne witness — his testimony is true, and he knows that he tells the truth — that you also may believe" (John 19:35). "This is the disciple who is bearing witness to these things, and who has written these things; and we know that his testimony is true" (John 21:24). Concerning his knowledge of Jesus, John affirmed in his first letter "that which was from the beginning, which we have heard, which we have seen with our eyes, which we have looked upon and touched with our hands, concerning the word of life — the life was made manifest, and we saw it, and testify to it, and proclaim to you the eternal life which was with the Father and was made manifest to us — that which we have seen and heard we proclaim also to you, so that you may have fellowship with us" (1 John 1:1-3). Luke claims contact with eyewitnesses (Luke 1:1-2).

Evidence for the authorship of the Gospels will be examined. Since the first Gospel was quoted by A.D. 110, we know it was written before that time, putting it within the lifetime of Matthew. Ignatius (A.D. 110), Polycarp (A.D. 110), the *Epistle of Barnabas* (A.D. 130), Justin Martyr (A.D. 140) and the *Didache* (A.D. 150) all quote from Matthew's Gospel. These four sources were written within the first fifty years of the second century.[2]

Two second-century statements identify Matthew as author of a record about Jesus. In A.D. 140 Papias, a student of the apostle John, said, "Matthew wrote the oracles in the Hebrew language."[3] Some say that the word for oracles (*logia*) could not refer to a Gospel. However, Papias used the same word when he referred to Mark's Gospel.[4] In A.D. 180 Irenaeus said, "Matthew also issued a written Gospel among the Hebrews in their own dialect."[5] We have no copy of a Hebrew or Aramaic original of Matthew's Gospel. The Gospel of Matthew in the Greek text does not appear to be translated from Aramaic. Why couldn't Matthew have published both a Greek and a Hebrew copy of his Gospel?

Unanimous second-century testimony identifies John Mark as the author of the second Gospel. In A.D. 140 Papias said, "The presbyter [the apostle John] said, 'Mark, having become the interpreter of Peter, wrote down accurately . . . whatsoever he remembered of the things said or done by Christ.'"[6] Justin Martyr, also in A.D. 140, referred to the statement in Mark 3:17 as in the "Memoirs of Peter."[7] The *Anti-Marcionite Prologue* (A.D. 160) said, "Mark . . . was the interpreter of Peter. After the death of Peter himself he wrote down this same Gospel in the regions of Italy."[8] In A.D. 180 Irenaeus affirmed, "Mark, the disciple and interpreter of Peter, did also hand down to us in writing what had been preached by Peter."[9]

The early evidence is strong and unanimous that Luke wrote the third Gospel. Justin Martyr in his Dialogue with Trypho twice quoted the Gospel of Luke (A.D. 140).[10] The *Anti-Marcionite Prologue* (about A.D. 160) identified the author of the third Gospel and the Acts of the Apostles as the physician and companion of Paul. The *Muratorian Canon* (A.D. 170) recorded, "The third book of the Gospels Luke compiled in his own name from reports, the physician whom Paul took with him after the Ascension of Christ, as it were for a traveling companion."[11] In A.D. 180, Irenaeus wrote, "Luke also, the companion of Paul, recorded in a book the Gospel preached by him."[12] He called Luke "the follower and disciple of the apostles"[13] and said "Luke was inseparable from Paul, . . . his fellow-labourer in the Gospel."[14]

Unbelieving critics strongly attacked the fourth Gospel because it so clearly presents the deity of Jesus. Some dated it late in the second century. Yet we have evidence of the early existence of the book. Ignatius in A.D. 110 did not directly quote the book but made allusions that seem to be dependent on the fourth Gospel. The oldest copy of any part of the New Testament is the *John Rylands Fragment* [𝔓 (*papyrus*), 52] that contains a few verses from John 18. It was copied about A.D. 125 and was found in Egypt. This proves that John's Gospel was in use in Egypt early in the second century.

The *Muratorian Canon* (A.D. 170) said, "The fourth book of the Gospel is that of John, one of the disciples." It stated that no disagreement existed between the four accounts because all were written "under the one guiding Spirit." After quoting 1 John 1:1, it stated John "professed to be not only an eyewitness but also a hearer and narrator of all the wonderful things of the Lord."[15] Irenaeus, writing in A.D. 180, said, "Afterwards [after the writing of the first three Gospels], John, the disciple of the Lord, who also had leaned upon his breast, did himself publish a Gospel during his residence at Ephesus in Asia."[16] Irenaeus was a disciple of Polycarp who was a disciple of the apostle John. Clement of Alexandria

(A.D. 190) also voiced this view, "Last of all John, perceiving that the external facts had been made plain in the Gospels, being urged by his friends and inspired by the Spirit, composed a spiritual Gospel."[17]

TESTIMONY TO THE
AUTHORSHIP OF THE GOSPELS

MATTHEW

	A.D. 140	Papias
	A.D. 180	Irenaeus

MARK

	A.D. 140	Papias
	A.D. 140	Justin Martyr
	A.D. 160	*Anti-Marcionite Prologue*
	A.D. 180	Irenaeus

LUKE

	A.D. 140	Justin Martyr
	A.D. 160	*Anti-Marcionite Prologue*
	A.D. 170	*Muratorian Canon*
	A.D. 180	Irenaeus

JOHN

	A.D. 170	*Muratorian Canon*
	A.D. 180	Irenaeus
	A.D. 190	Clement of Alexandria

In historical studies one accepts the claimed author of a book unless compelling evidence from the time of its production refutes it. No such evidence exists to refute traditional authorship of any of the four Gospels. The clear evidence supports the claimed authors.

Letters provide valuable historical evidence because people most fully reveal their personal thoughts and feelings in letters. In addition to the evidence in the Gospels the letters of Paul provide one of the earliest sources for our knowledge about Christianity. Though critics dispute a few of Paul's letters, most of them are acknowledged as written by Paul between A.D. 50 and A.D. 65. Paul claimed to be an eyewitness of the risen Christ (1 Corinthians 15:8).

The New Testament books were written between A.D. 50 and A. D. 100. The time lapse between the life of Jesus and these writings is very short compared with that of other books about persons from the Greek and Roman world. Several individuals wrote about Jesus in books written separately and circulated separately. Paul Barnett stated:

> Because the parts were produced separately and independently, we have a number of built-in means of checking one against the other. Since there are seven or eight independently written accounts which refer to Jesus, it is as reasonable to believe he existed as it is to believe a road accident happened because seven or eight people independently said it did. The evidence for Christ is to be accepted or rejected in much the same way a judge and jury accept or reject evidence from witnesses to an accident or a crime.[18]

We can trust the New Testament books as sources written by men who either knew Jesus directly or gained information from eyewitnesses.

Copied Correctly?

Historians are interested in the authorship of a source and they also seek to answer the question, "Has the written text been copied correctly through the years?" Many old manuscripts show how accurately the biblical books have been copied through the centuries.

The New Testament books apparently were originally written on papyrus. Papyrus was a writing material made from reeds that grew along the Nile River. The reed was split open, criss-crossed and pounded together to make a writing material. Papyrus was not as durable as some writing materials because moisture caused it to disintegrate. Evidence from the language used in everyday papyri writings discovered by archaeologists has conclusively demonstrated that the New Testament books were written during the first century.

The earliest copy of any part of the New Testament available to scholars is the *John Rylands Fragment* (𝔓 52). This scrap of papyrus contains verses from John 18:31-33 and 36-37 and was copied about A.D. 125.

Another manuscript, the *Bodmer Papyrus* (𝔓 66), contains the first fourteen chapters of John and fragments from the last seven chapters. Another papyrus manuscript from the Bodmer collection (𝔓 72) is our earliest copy of Jude and 1 and 2 Peter. Yet another Bodmer manuscript (𝔓 75) contains the Gospels of Luke and John. These were copied around A.D. 200.

In 1930 a discovery was made of a collection of New Testament books on papyrus in three parts, the *Chester Beatty Papyri*. One part contained the Gospels and Acts, the second contained nine of Paul's letters and the third contained the book of Revelation. They were copied between A.D. 200 and A.D. 250 (𝔓 45, 𝔓 46, 𝔓 47).

An important discovery was made at Mt. Sinai in May, 1844, by a German Bible scholar, Lobegott Konstantine Tischendorf. In the monastery of St. Catherine at the foot of Mt. Sinai, Tischendorf discovered several sheets of a very old Greek Old Testament in a wastebasket. The material from the baskets was used to start fires. He was allowed to take 43 sheets but then he said, "The too lively satisfaction which I had displayed had aroused their suspicion as to the value of this manuscript." The monastery's authorities refused to allow him to take the rest of the pages.

He returned in 1853 but did not find this manuscript. On a third visit in February of 1859 as Tischendorf was ready to give up his search, the steward of the monastery showed him a Greek Bible. It included the Old Testament pages he was refused 15 years before, more of the Old Testament and the entire New Testament. Tischendorf described his reaction,

The Sinaitic Manuscript of the Bible in
Greek found by Tischendorf at Mt. Sinai in 1844.

Inscription found in 1961 at Caesarea mentioning the
names of the emperor Tiberius and the governor Pontius Pilate.

"Full of joy which this time I had the self-command to conceal from the steward and the rest of the community, I asked, as if in a careless way, for permission to take the manuscript to my sleeping chamber, to look over more at leisure."[19]

He gained possession of the manuscript and presented it to the Russian Emperor. In 1933, the British Museum purchased it for almost one-half million dollars. This Sinaitic Manuscript and another manuscript of comparable value, the Vatican Manuscript, are both complete New Testaments. They were copied on parchment (writing material made from treated animal skins) between A.D. 300 and A.D. 350. They are valuable early witnesses to the New Testament text. These may be two of the fifty parchment Bibles the Emperor Constantine ordered from Eusebius of Caesarea in A.D. 332.

The Dead Sea Scrolls have been called "the greatest manuscript discovery of modern times." Though they do not contain New Testament books, they provide evidence that the Old Testament has been carefully copied. In March 1947, an Arab shepherd looking for a lost goat found some jars containing leather scrolls in a cave northwest of the Dead Sea. This led to the finding of hundreds of scrolls. The Essenes, a monastic sect of the Jews, had hidden their scriptures and other writings in these caves about A.D. 71 before the Roman army arrived and destroyed their Qumran settlement. These writings remained untouched in these caves for almost 1900 years.

Manuscripts were found of most Old Testament books. One of the most important finds was a complete copy of Isaiah (Isaiah A). This twenty-four foot leather scroll may be the earliest copy we have of a complete book of the Bible. Many other scrolls of Bible books were found in the caves. Scholars, liberal and conservative alike, agree that these scrolls were copied about 100 B.C.

Here is a good test to see how accurately the book of Isaiah has been copied. Before 1947, our earliest text of Isaiah had been copied about A.D. 900. The Dead Sea scrolls of Isaiah were copied 1000 years before that manuscript. How closely do these two texts compare? Gleason Archer, Professor of Old Testament at Trinity Evangelical Divinity School, stated that the two Isaiah scrolls, "proved to be word for word identical with our standard Hebrew Bible in more than 95% of the text. The five per cent of variation consisted chiefly of obvious slips of the pen and variations in spelling." [20]

The Dead Sea Scrolls give evidence that the Old Testament had been copied accurately. The Dead Sea Scrolls and the Greek version of the Old Testament, the Septuagint, prove conclusively that the Old Testament was in existence over 100 years before Christ. This is important when we study Christ's fulfillment of Old Testament prophecies.

Notice, by contrast, the limited manuscript evidence for other ancient books. Herodotus wrote his *History* about 425 B.C. The earliest existing copy is from A.D. 900. That is a time span of 1300 years. Only eight copies are in existence. Aristotle wrote *Poetics* about 322 B.C. The earliest existing copy is from A.D. 1100. In this instance the time span is 1400 years, with only five copies in existence.

Josephus wrote *Jewish War* shortly after A.D. 70. We have only nine complete manuscripts. The earliest is a fifth century Latin translation. The eight Greek manuscripts are from the tenth century or later.

TEXTUAL EVIDENCE
FOR THE GREEK AND JEWISH CLASSICS

Source	Date Written	Earliest Manuscript	Number of Manuscripts
Herodotus, *History*	425 B.C.	A.D. 900	8
Aristotle, *Poetics*	322 B.C.	A.D. 1100	5
Josephus, *Jewish War*	A.D. 70	A.D. 900	8

We have far superior evidence that the New Testament has been correctly copied than we have for the Greek and Roman classics. F.F. Bruce, who at one time taught the classics in a British university until he started teaching the New Testament, states, "There is no body of ancient literature in the whole world which enjoys such a wealth of good textual attestation as the New Testament." In comparing the evidence for the text of the New Testament with that for the Greek and Roman classics, Bruce observed, "But the textual evidence for the New Testament is abundant beyond comparison with these other works."[21] Stephen Neill and Tom Wright agreed, "We have a far better and more reliable text of the New Testament than of any other ancient work whatever."[22]

From the beginning of the church, Christians regularly assembled on Sundays. "The 'habit' of meeting accompanied as it was by public scripture reading led to the proliferation and therefore the preservation of the scriptures."[23] Barnett stated:

> When Josephus and Tacitus completed their manuscripts there was no immediate system for either preserving or copying what they had written. With the New Testament it was different. That collection of books became the much-copied Scriptures of a rapidly growing movement which soon became the state religion. Those Scriptures in turn gave rise to an immense output of early Christian literature which quoted them at great length and, in effect, preserved them. [24]

The evidence of Greek manuscripts of the New Testament books gives strong support to the correctness of the copying of the text of the New Testament. We have over 5000 Greek manuscripts (many complete, others partial) of the New Testament. The text of the New Testament has also been preserved in the quotations of the early Christian writers. A British writer, Sir David Dalrymple, said, "I possessed all the existing works of the Fathers of the second and third centuries. I commenced to search, and up to this time I have found the entire New Testament, except eleven verses."[25] Of these quotations of the New Testament in early Christian writing, Bruce Metzger of Princeton Theological Seminary observed, "They would be sufficient alone for the reconstruction of practically the entire New Testament."[26]

The evidence includes Greek manuscripts (whole or in part) totaling over 5000, including one fragment from A.D. 125, most of the New Testament by A.D. 250 and two complete New Testaments by A.D. 325; most of the New Testament is quoted in early Christian books by A.D. 400; the Old Latin and Syriac translations dating from the second century give another line of evidence.

TEXTUAL EVIDENCE FOR THE NEW TESTAMENT

Greek Manuscripts — (whole or partial) 5,000+

A.D. 125	John Rylands Fragment (few verses from John 18)
A.D. 250	Bodmer and Chester Beatty Manuscripts (most of New Testament)
A.D. 325	Sinaitic and Vatican Manuscripts (two complete New Testaments)

Quotations in Early Christian Writings

A.D. 96 to 400	Most of the New Testament Quoted

Translations — New Testament into Two Other Languages

A.D. 150	Into Old Latin and Old Syriac

In the thousands of manuscripts, understandably many variations are found. B.F. Westcott and F.J.A. Hort, two authorities on the New Testament text, noted that the portion of our New Testament which is in doubt, whether it was in the original or not, would amount to only one-half of a page in a five-hundred-page Greek New Testament. They are speaking only of variations that affect meaning.[27]

We can be confident that what we read in the New Testament is what the original writers wrote. We do not have the handwritten originals signed by the New Testament writers. Yet we have access to the truth written in the original because the copies are almost exactly like the originals.

J.W. McGarvey, New Testament scholar, told of a gentleman who left a large estate to his grandchildren. The estate was not to be divided among the grandchildren until all were twenty-one years of age. Many copies of the will were circulated. Some were copies of copies. The original copy of the will was destroyed when the lawyer's office burned. At the time of the division of the property a lawyer found that no two copies of the will were exactly alike. All known copies of the will were examined. They found differences in grammar, in spelling, even in numbers. None of the variations affected the rights of the heirs. In essentials the wills were precisely the same. The estate was divided to the satisfaction of all.[28] Copyist variations in the manuscripts of the Bible have not obscured the message of the Bible.

Evidence supports the integrity and genuineness of the New Testament books. The actual authors of the New Testament books are the authors claimed by the New Testament and early Christians. Their writings have been copied correctly through the centuries. *The New Testament Stands True as History.*

Chapter Two
THE NEW TESTAMENT STANDS TRUE AS HISTORY

PART 2 — HISTORICAL ACCURACY

In seeking to know God we must consider the historical credentials of the books that tell about the One who claimed to come from God. Can we trust the New Testament as a reliable historical record?

Some people say they can be Christians even if the New Testament is not historically reliable. If the history of the New Testament is false, then Christianity is false. A cartoon showed two men on a teeter-totter. The man on the end that extended out over a steep cliff had a gun. He shot and killed the man who was over the safe end of the teeter-totter, but then plunged to his own death on the rocks below. If we cannot accept the New Testament as factual, we end up destroying true Christian faith, in effect committing spiritual suicide. Paul said, "If Christ be not raised from the dead our faith is futile" (1 Corinthians 15:17).

As history, the New Testament stands true. The evidence presented in chapter one shows we can have confidence that the actual authors of the New Testament books were the authors claimed by the books and by early writers. These books have been copied correctly through the centuries. Next we need to consider the question, "Are the books historically true?"

Marks of Reliability

Common sense marks of reliability help in testing the evidence for the reliability of a historical source: honest writers, competent writers, several writers, consistent testimony, and confirmed testimony.

MARKS OF RELIABILITY

1) Honesty of Witnesses
2) Competence of Witnesses
3) Several Witnesses
4) Consistency in Testimony
5) External Confirmation

Evidence supports the honesty of the New Testament writers. Many Christians died under Roman persecution rather than deny their testimony. Why would they die for what they knew to be a lie? A person might be deceived and die for a falsehood. But the apostles were in a position to know the facts about Jesus' resurrection and they still died for it. Their writings have had the greatest power to make men honest. It is difficult to believe that they are frauds themselves.

Were the writers of the New Testament records competent?

The New Testament books are well organized and well-written books. There is no evidence of derangement, deception, or hallucination on the part of the writers.

Luke, physician and traveling companion with the apostle Paul, wrote Luke and Acts. These books make up one-fourth of the New Testament and one-half of the historical material in the New Testament. In the first four verses of his Gospel Luke stated his sources of information, his historical method and his purpose for writing. Luke introduced his book in a way similar to that of the classical Greek historians, for example, Polybius.

Luke identified his sources, "Inasmuch as many have undertaken to compile a narrative of the things which have been accomplished among us, just as they were delivered to us by those who from the beginning were eyewitnesses and ministers of the word. . ." (Luke 1:1-2). Luke listed both primary and secondary sources. Historians prize primary sources because they constitute the most direct source of information. Of the eyewitnesses Luke interviewed, one may have been Mary. Luke described the birth and childhood of Jesus from Mary's point of view. While Paul was imprisoned at Caesarea before going to Rome, Luke could have gone to Nazareth and talked with Mary. "Ministers of the word" probably refers to the apostles. (See Acts 6:4.) Luke did not identify the short accounts nor did he criticize them. He suggested that he could give a more comprehensive picture.

Luke then described his historical method, ". . . It seemed good to me also, having followed all things closely from some time past, to write an orderly account for you most excellent Theophilus . . ." (Luke 1:3). The word translated "having followed" is similar to our word for research. "Closely" could be translated "accurately." "An orderly account" indicates careful organization in his narrative. So Luke said he researched the facts; he tested them for accuracy; and he wrote an orderly account.

Of Luke's historical method stated in Luke 1:1-4, historian Earle E. Cairns affirmed, "No better summary of the best elements of modern historical method can be found in the accepted modern manuals on historical method."[1]

Modern books on historical method suggest the following steps in the writing of history. First is research; you collect all relevant data. Next is the criticism step where evaluation is made of the data, separating fact from fiction. Last is the composition of the narrative where the material is arranged in an orderly presentation. Luke followed this preferred historical method.

Luke stated his purpose, ". . . that you may know the truth concerning the things of which you have been informed" (Luke 1:4). The last word in Luke's long Greek sentence (1:1-4) is the word "truth." Luke wanted his readers to know with reliability and certainty the truth about Jesus of Nazareth. He purposed to write a true record.

MODERN HISTORICAL METHOD

1) Research — Collection of Data
2) Criticism — Establish Accuracy of Data
3) Composition — Orderly Arrangement of Material

Our knowledge of Jesus of Nazareth does not depend upon one person or one source. We have the life of Jesus written by four writers. At least four other writers record their testimony about Christianity in the New Testament. Most were eyewitnesses of Jesus.

The New Testament records are consistent in their testimony to the facts about Jesus Christ. We encounter the usual difficulties common in true testimony from many witnesses. *Yet no author denies what another affirms!*

LUKE AS HISTORIAN

Sources — (Luke 1:1-2)

Primary Sources	"Eyewitnesses"
	"Ministers of the Word"
Secondary Sources	"Narratives"

Method — (Luke 1:3)

Researched Facts	"having followed"
Established Accuracy	"closely" [accurately]
Orderly Narrative	"orderly account"

Purpose — (Luke 1:4)

True Record	"truth"

In a college speech class, the teacher said, "The Bible is full of historical blunders."

My wife was a student in that class. She raised her hand and asked, "Could you give us an example?"

The teacher grew flustered and said, "Don't call me on the carpet. I don't know the examples but I have heard that all my life." It is much easier to accuse the Bible of error than to establish such. The Bible has stood true even in the face of centuries of criticism.

Kenneth Kantzer, educator and former editor of *Christanity Today*, discussed the problem of apparent contradiction in true testimony,

> Some time ago the mother of a dear friend of ours was killed. We first learned of her death through a trusted mutual friend who reported that our friend's mother had been standing on the street corner waiting for a bus, had been hit by another bus passing by, was fatally injured, and died a few minutes later. Shortly thereafter, we learned from the grandson of the dead woman that she had been involved in a collision, was thrown from the car in which she was riding, and was killed instantly. The boy was quite certain of his facts, relayed them clearly, and stated that he had secured his information directly from his mother — the daughter of the woman who had been killed. No further information was forthcoming from either source. Which would you believe?
>
> We trusted both of our friends, but we certainly could not assemble the data in a single sequence. Much later, upon further inquiry, we were able to talk to our friend and her son in our living room. There, quietly and slowly, we probed for a harmonization. We learned that the grandmother had been waiting for a bus, was hit by another bus, and was critically injured. She had been picked up by a passing car to rush her to the hospital —but in the haste, the car in which she was being transported to the hospital collided with another car. She was thrown from the car and died instantly. I submit that this story from my own experience presents no greater difficulty than that of any recorded in the Gospels, not even excepting the two divergent accounts of the death of Judas.
>
> Such coincidences occur repeatedly; they are inherent in independent accounts of any event. The only significant difference between this story and the accounts of the four Evangelists is the fact that we cannot cross-examine the Gospel witnesses. We live 2,000 years too late. [2]

39

Not only do the New Testament records have a consistent testimony, but evidence from outside the New Testament confirms their testimony. The New Testament records square with factual knowledge of the first century Greek-Roman world. In history, as well as in a court of law, confirmation from independent and converging lines of evidence helps to establish the validity of testimony. In the first century the believers and unbelievers who were eyewitnesses to many Gospel facts provided a check on the accuracy of the early preaching and writing.

Confirmation from Archaeology

Confirmation from archaeology provides another important line of external evidence. Agatha Christie, a British novelist, told an interviewer there was an advantage being married to an archaeologist because the older you got the more he was interested in you! Archaeology is the study of the material remains from ancient civilizations. Archaeological research has done much to strengthen confidence in the historical reliability of both the Old Testament and the New Testament.

When William Ramsay attended a British university he was taught the book of Acts was not written by Luke and was not historically reliable. It was fiction written about A.D. 160 to patch up a quarrel in the early church between Peter and Paul. After more than thirty years of archaeological research in Asia Minor and other Bible lands, Ramsay stated his view of Luke, "Luke is a historian of the first rank. . . . Luke's history is unsurpassed in respect of its trustworthiness."[3]

Though he was prejudiced against Luke, the stubborn facts made a believer out of him. Archaeologists have discovered ruins confirming the existence of the Pool of Bethesda in Jerusalem where Jesus healed the lame man (John 5:2). Jacob's well is in the modern city of Nablus. It was here that Jesus talked to the woman at the well (John 4:6). Ruins have been uncovered in Capernaum of a first-century synagogue where Jesus worshiped and performed many miracles.

In 1961 at Caesarea in the ruins of a Roman theater was found an inscription that mentioned the names of the Emperor Tiberius and the Governor Pilate. This incidental evidence confirms the New Testament picture of the political relationship between these men.

Archaeology has thrown light on the story of the Jews who got angry with Paul because they assumed that he had brought a Gentile into the temple area (Acts 21:29). A complete inscription was found in 1871 and a fragment in 1938 giving warning about bringing Gentiles into the temple. "No foreigner may enter within the fence and enclosure around the temple. Whoever is caught will have himself to thank for his death which will follow." Josephus also mentions such a warning.

Statements about the cities of the first century world would be a place where errors would be obvious if the New Testament were not reliable. What the New Testament affirms harmonizes with facts from archaeology and ancient history. Athens was a city questing for new ideas. Mars Hill can be visited today where Paul preached about "The Unknown God" (Acts 17:23). He mentioned he had seen an inscription bearing these words. A similar inscription from nearby Pergamum on a stone altar read "to unknown gods."

In Corinth, a marble inscription on a pavement near the city theater read, "Erastus, Administrator of Public Buildings laid this pavement at his own expense." Paul in his letter to the Romans, written from Corinth, sends greetings from "Erastus, the city Treasurer" (Romans 16:23). The Erastus of the inscription may have been Paul's friend. When Paul was in Ephesus, the silversmith opposed him because he spoke against idolatry. The people cried for two hours in a theater, "Great is the goddess, Diana." Although the ruins of a theater in Ephesus date from a later period than Paul, earlier evidence beneath these ruins reveals the worship of Diana and the regular meeting of the Judgment Council that fits the picture of the Acts record (Acts 19:23-41).

Luke has been accused of error in his titles of officials. Archaeological research has confirmed Luke's accuracy in calling Gallio "proconsul of Achaia" (Acts 18:12), Sergius Paulus "proconsul of Cyprus" (Acts 13:7), the chief official of Malta as the "first man of the island" (Acts 28:7), and Ephesus as "the temple keeper" of Artemis (Acts 19:35). Luke called the officials of Thessalonica politarchs, which literally means "city rulers" (Acts 17:6). Critics said that Luke was wrong because this title was not found in the classical historians. However, five inscriptions have been found which refer to the politarchs of Thessalonica thus proving Luke right in calling the city officials "politarchs."

F.F. Bruce pointed to Luke's "ability to use the right technical title for the right official in one place after another throughout the provinces of the Roman Empire" as "one of the most impressive features of Luke's detailed accuracy."[4] F.F. Bruce also observed, "Where Luke has been suspected of inaccuracy, and accuracy has been vindicated by some inscriptional evidence, it may be legitimate to say that archaeology has confirmed the New Testament record."[5]

Nelson Glueck, the late Jewish President of Hebrew Union Seminary in Cincinnati, spent over 40 summers in archaeological research in Palestine and Jordan. He acknowledged, "No archaeological discovery has ever controverted [proven false] a biblical reference."[6] On the same page he said that archaeology cannot prove the inspiration of the Bible, but it does support its historical accuracy where it has been tested.

Confirmation of the central facts of the Gospel story comes from Jewish and pagan historians. Josephus was a Jewish historian who wrote near the end of the first century. Current texts of Josephus' writings contain a disputed passage about Jesus. Setting this controversial text aside, Josephus bears witness to Jesus existing in the early part of the first century, to His being the brother of James the Just and His being called the Christ.[7] Rabbi Eliezer also represents the Jewish view of Jesus at the end of the first century. He does not name Jesus but said, ". . . There was a man born of women, who should rise up and seek to make himself God and to cause the whole world to go astray. . . . And if he says that he is God he is a liar, and he will deceive and say that he

NON-CHRISTIAN
HISTORICAL EVIDENCE ABOUT JESUS

Source	Date of Writing	Facts recorded
Jewish Sources		
Josephus	A.D. 70-100	He was called "the Christ." His brother was James.
Eliezer	A.D. 90-100	He claimed to be God and that he would depart and return.
Babylonian Talmud		Jesus (Yeshu) worked magic and led Israel astray and was hanged on Passover eve.
Roman Sources		
Tacitus	A.D. 100	Christ was executed in Judea when Tiberius was emperor (A.D. 14-37) and when Pontius Pilate was governor (A.D. 26-36).
Pliny	A.D. 112	His followers worshiped Him as (a) god.
Tacitus & Pliny	A.D. 100/112	His followers were called Christians. They were numerous in Rome and Bithynia.

departeth and cometh again at the end."[8] *The Babylonian Talmud* said, "On the Eve of Passover Jeshu was hanged. . . . he has practiced sorcery and enticed Israel to apostasy."[9] Apparently this refers to Jesus of Nazareth as he is referred to as "Yeshu" in other Talmudic passages. This Jewish reference was not intended to convey historical information but were rather expressions of derision. The Roman historian Tacitus, about A. D. 100 said, "Christus . . . was put to death by Pontius Pilate, procurator of Judea in the reign of Tiberius."[10] Tacitus said Nero blamed the burning of Rome on the multitude of people called Christians. Pliny of Bithynia in A.D. 112 said in a letter to the emperor that the numerous Christians in his province "sang in alternate verse a hymn to Christ as to a god."[11]

While the evidence from Jewish and secular historians is limited, it does give independent confirmation of some of the historical facts about Jesus of Nazareth.

To find information about Alexander the Great, we look in an encyclopedia. But where did the authors of the encyclopedia article get their information? During Alexander's lifetime the *Royal Journal* was written, under Alexander's supervision, documenting his accomplishments. Callisthenes, a journalist who traveled with Alexander, wrote about him. Callisthenes was related to Aristotle who had been Alexander's teacher. After Alexander's death two of his generals, Ptolemy and Aristobulus, wrote biographies about their leader. About one hundred years after Alexander's death, some romances were written which deified Alexander, making him a Greek god. About the same time the Peripatetics, who had been influenced by Aristotle's later dislike for Alexander, pictured Alexander as a drunkard. Historians writing 300-500 years after Alexander's death wrote about him. They include Diodorus, Justin, Arrian, Curtius, and Plutarch. Arrian, a major source for our knowledge of Alexander, wrote about A. D. 130.[12]

How many of these sources do we have available for study today? When Alexander was in India, a fire destroyed the *Royal Journal*. Callisthenes was caught in a plot against

Alexander's life. Callisthenes was executed and all his writings burned. No copies of the books written by the two generals have survived. Only fragments of the romances and the writings of the Peripatetics have been preserved by the later historians. Our knowledge of Alexander the Great is based on history books written 300-500 years after his death. That is a long time after the events!

SOURCES FOR KNOWLEDGE
ABOUT ALEXANDER THE GREAT

Source Written	Sources Available Today
During His Lifetime Royal Journal Callisthenes	Not Available
After His Death Generals: Ptolemy Aristobulus	Not Available
About 100 Years Later Romances Peripatetics	Only fragments of these
Historians – 300 to 500 years *After His Death* Diodorus Justin Arrian Curtius Plutarch	These histories are available

We have far better sources for our knowledge of Jesus of Nazareth. We have written testimony of at least six eyewitnesses to Jesus (Matthew, John, Paul, Peter, James, and Jude). Some were written within twenty years after His death. All were published within 70 years of His death. Luke said he gained information from eyewitnesses. Mark received information from Peter, an eyewitness. No time elapsed for legends to develop. They openly preached and published their writings while eyewitnesses were alive who could refute them if they spoke or wrote falsehood.

SOURCES FOR KNOWLEDGE OF JESUS

Eyewitnesses:

Matthew
John
Paul
Peter
James
Jude

*(Written testimony 20-70
years after His death)*

Researchers Who Interviewed Eyewitnesses:

Mark
Luke

*(Written testimony 20-40
years after His Death)*

The New Testament Stands True As History!

Jesus healed the paralyzed man who was
let down through the roof by his friends.

The Garden Tomb, possible site of
the burial and resurrection of Jesus.

"Before Abraham was, I am." *John 8:58*

"I and the Father are one." *John 10:30*

"I am the way, and the truth, and the life; no one comes to the Father, but by me."   *John 14:6*

" 'That you may know that the Son of Man has authority on earth to forgive sins,' he said to the paralytic, 'I say to you, rise, take up your pallet and go home.' "   *Mark 2:10*

"If I am not doing the works of my Father, then do not believe me; but if I do them, even though you do not believe me, believe the works, that you may know and understand that the Father is in me, and I am in the Father."   *John 10:37-38*

"If Christ has not been raised, then your faith is futile and you are still in your sins . . . . But in fact Christ has been raised from the dead."   *1 Corinthians 15:17,20*

"A man who was merely a man and said the sort of things Jesus said would not be a great moral teacher. He would be either a lunatic — on a level with the man who says he is a poached egg or else he would be the Devil of Hell. You must make your choice: Either this man was and is the Son of God: or else a madman or something worse. You can shut Him up for a fool; you can spit at Him and kill Him as a demon; or you can fall at his feet and call him Lord and God. But let us not come with any patronizing nonsense about His being a great human teacher. He has not left that open to us. He did not intend to."   *C. S. Lewis*

Chapter Three
JESUS STANDS TRUE AS THE SON OF GOD

PART 1 — CLAIMS TO DEITY

Strong historical evidence demonstrates that the New Testament records stand true as accurate history. If we accept the New Testament books as reliable historical records, then we must make a judgment about the claims and credentials of Jesus of Nazareth.

A small girl had been put to bed. Lightning flashed. Thunder clapped. A cry came out of her room, "Mommy!"

Her mother hurrying in asked, "What's the matter?"

"I'm scared!" was the response. After calming her by assuring her that God would take care of her, the mother left the room. Again lightning flashed and thunder shook the house.

"Mommy!" came the pleading call.

The mother came and looked at her scared child, "Didn't I tell you that God loves you? He'll take care of you."

"Yes, Mommy, but I want someone near me who has skin on him!"

Because human beings have difficulty comprehending God, it is wonderful that God stepped down "with skin on Him" in Jesus Christ to reveal God to man.

A German girl asked her mother, "Where is God?"

Her mother responded, "God is everywhere."

The girl answered, "I don't want God everywhere. I want Him, *someone, somewhere.*" Jesus was God stepping down in the person of "someone, somewhere" to show Himself to man.

To the paralyzed man let down through the roof Jesus announced, "Man, your sins are forgiven you." The scribes and Pharisees questioned, "*Who is this* that speaks blasphemies?" (Luke 5:20-21). When Jesus granted pardon to the sinful woman in the house of Simon the Pharisee, those at the table remarked, "*Who is this,* who even forgives sins?" (Luke 7:49). After Jesus stilled the storm on the sea, the disciples exclaimed, "*Who then is this,* that even wind and sea obey him?" (Mark 4:41). Jesus rode a donkey into the city of Jerusalem to the acclaim of the crowds. "All the city was stirred, saying, *Who is this?*" (Matthew 21:10, emphasis added).

During the last year of His earthly ministry, Jesus asked His disciples what people were saying about who He was. They said, "Some say John the Baptist, others say Elijah, and others Jeremiah or one of the prophets." Then He faced them squarely with the issue of His identity, "Who do you say that I am?" Peter replied, "You are the Christ, the Son of the living God" (Matthew 16:13-16). During the last week before His death Jesus asked, "What do you think of the Christ? Whose son is he?" (Matthew 22:42).

The essential question is—"Who is Jesus?" This question demands a personal response. Each person must answer. It is an *all important* question. How a person answers will determine his purpose in life and decide his eternal destiny. It is the most important question any person will ever answer.

The issue is also *all inclusive.* Believing Jesus is the Son of God and submiting to Him as Lord influences every area of one's life. It changes one's thoughts, feelings, motives, dreams, words, and actions. The decision concerns not only this life but the life hereafter as well.

The issue concerning the identity of Jesus is not only all important and all inclusive, but it is also *all impelling.* If Jesus is the Son of God, then believers will give their all to submit to His Lordship, even being willing to die for Him. Commitment to Jesus as King is a driving dynamic that knows no equal in the world.

Throughout the centuries artists have wrestled with the question, "Who is Jesus?" The English rock opera, *Jesus Christ Superstar,* asked "Jesus Christ, Jesus Christ, who are you? What have you sacrificed? Jesus Christ, Superstar, Do you think you're what they say you are?" The question will not go away. Various responses have been made and are being made concerning Jesus.

As turkey vultures, the Pharisees watched Jesus' every word and action, ready to pounce on any flaw or misdeed. What was their response to Jesus? They rejected Him as a blasphemer. There are those today who reject Jesus as unworthy of their allegiance. They want to be the masters of their own fates.

Judas, one of Jesus' disciples, betrayed Him with a kiss. Today many professing Christians are betraying Jesus by their lives. A minister was moonlighting as a philosophy professor in a night class in a California state college. He stated in one lecture, "We can't really know anything about God. The most profound knowledge of God is that we can't know anything about God."

During the intermission in the class, a girl walked up to the teacher and said, "I used to believe in God, but I consider myself an existentialist now. What you said makes some sense to me. But how can you be a minister and say things like that?"

He responded, "What do you mean? Do you think I have to be a fundamentalist?"

"No, but what do you believe about Jesus Christ?" she questioned.

He shrugged his shoulders and said, "Well, we have to reinterpret a lot of things!" Many who claim to be Christians betray Christ with their lips and lives.

Pilate's response to Jesus was different. It was not direct rejection or betrayal, but he tried to avoid a decision about the issue. Fearing a riot, he washed his hands before the crowd, saying, "I am innocent of this man's blood, see to it yourselves" (Matthew 27:24). Many say, "I don't want to make a decision about Christ." They, with Pilate, think they can evade the issue. They think they can put off or avoid deciding what they really believe about Jesus of Nazareth.

If a man asks a woman to marry him, and she refuses to answer, her answer is "No." When Jesus calls for us to decide about His claims and we try to avoid deciding, at that point we have decided against Him. "Not to decide is to decide against Him."

RESPONSES TO JESUS

Rejection — Pharisees

Betrayal — Judas

Evasion — Pilate

Belief — Disciples

Every person needs to consider openly and honestly the claims and credentials of Jesus of Nazareth. This chapter will examine Jesus' claims to deity. The next chapter will investigate evidence of His credentials of deity.

In answering the question, "Who is Jesus?" we will consider what His enemies and friends said about Him and then what Jesus claimed for Himself.

What His Enemies Said

One's enemies often tell the unvarnished truth. What did Jesus' enemies say about Him? Pilate repeatedly told the Jewish leaders, "I find no crime in this man" (Luke 23:4, 14, 22). He offered to release Jesus. The Jews countered, "If you release this man, you are not Caesar's friend" (John 19:12). Pilate yielded to their demands but insisted on Jesus' innocence.

Judas by virtue of the three years that he spent with Jesus was in a position to know firsthand what life was like with Him. In wanting to justify his own actions, he would surely have had a stronger motivation than any of the other of Jesus' enemies to expose some fault in Jesus. Yet after he had betrayed his Lord, he cried out, "I have sinned in betraying innocent blood" (Matthew 27:4). The priests turned a cold, brutal shoulder to him and said, "What is that to us? See to it yourself." Attempting to undo the deed, he hurled the thirty pieces of silver down on the floor in the temple. Judas' testimony concerning Jesus was "Innocent" (Matthew 27:3-5).

The Pharisees, the ever-present faultfinders, criticized Jesus. They accused Him of breaking the Sabbath. He broke their legalistic, nit-picking rules but not God's intention for the keeping of the Sabbath. Their charge that He befriended sinners indicated no fault in Jesus but exposed their own lack of love.

Their basic objection was that Jesus was a blasphemer because He claimed to be God in the flesh. They sought to kill Him "because he not only broke the sabbath but also called God his own Father, making himself equal with God" (John 5:18). They understood His divine claims. They were right in that respect. If He were an ordinary man, He would have been a blasphemer. Careful consideration must be given to the evidence for His claims.

WHAT HIS ENEMIES SAID

Pilate: "I find no crime in this man."

Judas: "I have sinned in betraying innocent blood."

Pharisee: He is a blasphemer "because he not only broke the sabbath but also called God his Father, making himself equal with God." "You, being a man, make yourself God."

What His Friends Said

As Jews, those who followed Jesus were strong believers in one God. Yet they became convinced that Jesus was God in human form living among them.

When the angel Gabriel announced to Mary in Nazareth that she would bear a son named Jesus, Mary did not understand. The angel explained that the conception of this child would be of God's power and that the child would be the Son of God. She responded in a beautiful way, "Behold, I am the handmaid of the Lord; let it be to me according to your word" (Luke 1:38).

Mary would testify of her relative Elizabeth greeting her as "the mother of my Lord" (Luke 1:43); of the angels telling the shepherds that the newborn was "a Savior, who is Christ the Lord" (Luke 2:11); of old Simeon being now ready to die because he had seen the Lord's Christ (Luke 2:26-32); of the wise men who were led to Him supernaturally by a star seeking the "King of the Jews" (Matthew 2:1-11). Mary was convinced that Jesus was One who came from God.

If one were to approach that rugged wilderness preacher, John the Baptist, and ask him, "What do you believe about Jesus?" he would repeat these statements: "Behold the lamb of God, who takes away the sin of the world! . . . This is the Son of God" (John 1:29, 34).

When John the Baptist was in prison, he sent his disciples to ask Jesus, "Are you he who is to come, or shall we look for another?" Jesus pointed to evidences for His claims, "Go and tell John what you hear and see: the blind receive their sight and the lame walk, lepers are cleansed and the deaf hear, and the dead are raised up, and the poor have the good news preached to them" (Matthew 11:3-6). John's testimony is that "Jesus is the Lamb of the God and the Son of God."

Andrew brought his brother, Peter, to see Jesus by these words, "We have found the Messiah" (John 1:41).

Six months before Jesus' death, Peter confessed, "You are the Christ, the Son of the living God" (Matthew 16:16). Earlier he said, "You have the words of eternal life; and we have believed, and have come to know that you are the Holy One of God" (John 6:68-69). Yet in the courtyard of the high priest at the trial of Jesus, Peter three times denied that he even knew Jesus (Mark 14:66-72). "The Lord turned and looked at Peter." He remembered that Jesus had predicted his denial. "And he went out and wept bitterly" (Luke 22:61-62).

About seven weeks later at the feast of Pentecost, Peter boldly announced in the temple area to the Jews that God has raised Jesus from the dead and "that God has made him both Lord and Christ, this Jesus whom you crucified" (Acts 2:36). Peter spent the rest of his life proclaiming in sermons, letters, and personal witness that Jesus was the Son of God.

WHAT HIS FRIENDS SAID

Angels to Shepherds:	"A savior, who is Christ the Lord."
Simeon:	"The Lord's Christ."
Wisemen:	"King of the Jews."
John the Baptist:	"The lamb of God, who takes away the sin of the world." "This is the Son of God."
Andrew:	"The Messiah."
Peter:	"The Christ, the Son of the living God." "The Holy One of God." "Lord and Christ."
Paul:	"The Son of God." ". . . in him the whole fullness of deity dwells bodily."

Some skeptics demand the eye-witness testimony of unbe-lievers to the reality of Christ. The testimony of a former unbeliever is available. Saul of Tarsus, a brilliant, strong-willed Jew, thought he should destroy Christianity. He forced Christians to blaspheme and even killed them (Acts 8:3; 22:4; 26:9-11). What changed Saul from a persecutor to a preacher? He became convinced that Jesus was really alive from the dead. After his conversion, he boldly entered the Damascus synagogue proclaiming of Jesus, "He is the Son of God" (Acts 9:20).

In his letters as in his preaching Paul testified to the deity of Jesus. He wrote to the Romans that Jesus Christ our Lord was "designated Son of God in power according to the Spirit of holiness by his resurrection from the dead" (Romans 1:4). To the Colossians he affirmed, "For in him the whole fulness of deity dwells bodily" (Colossians 2:9).

What Jesus Claimed

In the investigation of the identity of a person, mere claims do not establish proof. But Christ's claims must be clearly understood before one can make a fair evaluation of the evidence for or against those claims. What did Christ claim for Himself? Imagine a young man about 30 years of age claiming to be God in the flesh. It would be very difficult to accept such claims. Jesus lived in a flesh body. He worked in His carpenter's shop. He got hungry and tired. Consider the force of His claims.

Jesus claimed equality with God the Father. He told the Jews in the temple area, "I and the Father are one" (John 10:30). The Jews wanted to stone Him for this blasphemy say-ing, "Because you, being a man, make yourself God" (John 10:33).

"I have come down from heaven, not to do my own will, but the will of him who sent me" (John 6:38). He claimed to have come from His existence in heaven to dwell for a time on earth.

WHAT JESUS CLAIMED

Equality with God — "I and the Father are one."

Came from Heaven — "I have come down from heaven, not to do my own will, but the will of him who sent me."

Always Existed — "Before Abraham was, I am."

Only Way to God — "I am the way, and the truth, and the life; no one comes to the Father, but by me."

Seeing Him Was Seeing God — "He who has seen me has seen the Father."

Exclusive Knowledge of God — "No one knows the Father except the Son and anyone to whom the Son chooses to reveal him."

He Could Raise the Dead — "I am the resurrection and the life."

Savior — "You will die in your sins unless you believe that I am he."

Judge — "The Father . . . has given all judgment to the Son."

Jesus claimed that He had always existed. He informed the Jews, "'Your father Abraham rejoiced that he was to see my day; he saw it and was glad.' The Jews then said to Him, 'You are not yet fifty years old, and have you seen Abraham?' Jesus said to them, 'Truly, truly, I say to you, before Abraham was, I am'" (John 8:56-58). The Jews again wanted to stone Him for the audacity of His identifying Himself with the word "I AM" — the designation for Jehovah God in the Old Testament.

Christ claimed to be the only way to God. "I am the way, and the truth, and the life; no one comes to the Father, but by me" (John 14:6).

Jesus claimed to reveal God. Philip said that if Jesus would just show them the Father, they would be satisfied. Jesus answered, "He who has seen me has seen the Father" (John 14:9).

Jesus claimed an exclusive knowledge of God. "No one knows the Father except the Son and any one to whom the Son chooses to reveal him" (Matthew 11:27). Jesus insisted that He alone could explain who God is.

Jesus could raise the dead. "I am the resurrection and the life" (John 11:25). He said he could give life to whom He willed and could call the dead back to life.

Jesus said we must believe in Him if we want eternal salvation. "For you will die in your sins unless you believe that I am he" — that is the Messiah, the Son of God (John 8:24).

He claimed to be the judge of our eternal destiny. "The Father . . . has given all judgment to the Son" (John 5:22). "For the Son of man . . . will repay every man for what he has done" (Matthew 16:27).

Either He is who He claims to be or He is not. Either these statements Jesus made are true or they are false. Some people, however, try to find a halfway position. They praise Jesus as a teacher but reject His divine claims.

In a college English Literature course a student was asked to give a report on the influence of the Bible in English literature. The report concluded, "Either the Bible is a true revelation from God or it should be rejected as a false book. Either Jesus is the Son of God or He should be rejected as an imposter."

After students made several comments, the teacher said she did not go to church anymore, but she had gone to Sunday School as a child. Expressing her view of Christ, she said, "I don't believe the miracles. I don't believe Jesus was the Son of God, but I do think Jesus was a great moral teacher." Then she moved to another topic.

A former atheist, C.S. Lewis, makes it clear why that view

cannot be accepted:

> A man who was merely a man and said the sort of things Jesus said would not be a great moral teacher. He would be either a lunatic — on a level with the man who says he is a poached egg or else he would be the Devil of Hell. You must make your choice: Either this man was, and is, the Son of God: or else a madman or something worse. You can shut Him up for a fool; you can spit at Him and kill Him as a demon; or you can fall at His feet and call Him Lord and God. But let us not come with any patronizing nonsense about his being a great human teacher. He has not left that open to us. He did not intend to.[1]

This is a powerful statement. A person must get on one side of the fence or the other. He must decide either for or

```
+-------------------------------+
|                               |
|          JESUS IS             |
|                               |
|           LIAR                |
|                               |
|          LUNATIC              |
|                               |
|             or                |
|                               |
|           LORD                |
|                               |
+-------------------------------+
```

against Jesus. Here are the options — either Jesus is a liar and deceiving us or He is a lunatic and was self-deceived or He is the Lord and deity that He claimed to be.

The historical records indicate that when people understood Jesus' claims, they could no longer remain fair-weather friends. Some experienced terror in His presence because of His supernatural power. Others bristled with hatred at His holiness. Yet some fell at His feet in adoration.

"Who is Jesus?" is a question that must be answered. Jesus claimed to be the Son of God. The next chapter will survey Jesus' credentials of deity which established that in fact *Jesus Stands True as the Son of God.*

Chapter Four
JESUS STANDS TRUE AS THE SON OF GOD

PART 2 — CREDENTIALS OF DEITY

Two skeptics, Gilbert West and George Lyttleton, attended England's Oxford University in the eighteenth century. They planned to disprove Christianity. West wanted to refute the resurrection of Christ. Lyttleton attempted to discredit Paul's conversion. Their studies convinced them that the Bible was the Word of God. West wrote a book defending the resurrection as a fact. Lyttleton produced a case for Christianity by showing the reality of Paul's conversion. In his book on the resurrection, West included this quotation in his preface, "Blame not before thou hast examined the truth."[1]

Christians cannot force people to believe in Jesus. But believers must challenge those they meet to honestly consider the evidence for the claims of Christ. Chapter three presented Jesus' claims to deity. This chapter will present His credentials of deity.

Fulfilled Prophecy

Fulfilled prophecy is one line of evidence supporting Jesus' claim to be the Son of God. Jesus fulfilled more than two hundred predictions, spoken hundreds of years before by the Old Testament prophets.

About 1500 years before Christ, God spoke through Moses, "I will raise up for them a prophet like you from among their brethren; and I will put my words in his mouth, and he shall speak to them all that I command him" (Deuteronomy 18:18). After the feeding of the 5,000 the people proclaimed Jesus to be "the prophet who is to come into the world!" (John 6:14). The apostles also identified Jesus as this predicted prophet (Acts 3:22-23).

King David made many striking predictions about Christ in Psalms he wrote 1,000 years before Christ. He said that the

FORTY-FIVE FULFILLED MESSIANIC PROPHECIES

Prophet/ Date of Writing			Prophecy	Fulfillment
Moses	Gen	3:15	Born of seed of woman	Gal 4:4
1450 BC	Gen	22:18	Descended from Abraham	Matt 1:1
	Gen	49:10	Of tribe of Judah	Luke 3:23, 33
	Deut	18:15	A prophet like Moses	Acts 3:20-22
David	Ps	16:10	Resurrected	Luke 24:6, 31, 34
1000 BC				Acts 2:31
	Ps	22:1	Cry as one forsaken by God	Matt 27:46
	Ps	22:7-8	Words of mockers	Matt 27:31, 39-44
	Ps	22:16	Feet and hands pierced	Luke 23:33; John 19:18; 20:25
	Ps	22:18	Lots cast for garments	Matt 27:35; John 19:23-24
	Ps	31:5	Committed spirit to Father	Luke 23:46
	Ps	35:11	Accused by false witnesses	Matt 26:59-61
	Ps	41:9	Betrayed by a friend	Matt 10:4; John 13:18-21
	Ps	69:4	Hated without cause	John 15:24-25
	Ps	69:8	Rejected by His brethren	John 7:3, 5
	Ps	69:9	Zeal for House of God	John 2:15-17
	Ps	69:21	Vinegar for thirst	Matt 27:34
	Ps	78:2	Taught in parables	Matt 21:12
	Ps	110:1, 4	Lord and priest	Luke 2:11; Heb 3:14; 5:5-6
			At the right hand of God	Heb 1:3
	Ps	118:22	Rejected by rulers	Matt 21:42
Isaiah	Isa	7:14	Virgin conception	Matt 1:18-23
730 BC			Called Emmanuel	

coming One would be Lord and priest (Psalm 110:1, 4); that He would have zeal for the house of God (69:9). Psalm 22 reads almost like a script for the events at the cross: the cry of being forsaken by God (22:1); the very words of some of the mockers (22:7, 8); hands and feet pierced (22:16); garments parted and lots cast for His clothing (22:18). David foretells

	Isa	9:1-2	Ministry in Galilee	Matt 4:12-13, 16-17, 23
	Isa	11:1	Family of Jesse	Luke 3:23, 32
	Isa	11:2	Spirit upon Him (42:1)	Matt 3:16-17; John 3:34
	Isa	35:5-6	Worked miracles	Matt 11:4-6
	Isa	40:3	Voice in wilderness prepared way	Matt 3:1-2
	Isa	40:9	Would come as God	John 10:30
	Isa	49:6	Brought light to Gentiles	Acts 13:47
	Isa	53:3	Rejected by own people	John 1:11; 7:5, 48
	Isa	53:5-6	Wounded and spit upon	Matt 26:67
	Isa	53:7	Did not answer accusers	Matt 26:63; 27:12-19
	Isa	53:9	Buried in rich man's tomb	Matt 27;57-60
			Without guile	1Pet 2:22
	Isa	53:12	Killed with thieves	Matt 27:38, 50
			Numbered with transgressors	Mark 15:27-28
			Interceded for transgressors	Luke 23:34
Micah 710 BC	Micah	5:2	Birth in Bethlehem	Matt 2:1
Jeremiah 600 BC	Jer	23:5	Of house of David	Luke 3:23, 31; Acts 13:23
Zechariah 490 BC	Zech	9:9	Entered Jerusalem as king on donkey	Luke 19:35-37; Matt 21:5
		11:12	Sold for 30 pieces of silver	Matt 26:15
		11:13	Money thrown into Temple	Matt 27:3-5
			Money purchased potter's field	Matt 27:7
		12:10	Side pierced	John 19:34, 37
Daniel 530 BC	Dan	7:13-14	Called Son of man	John 12:34; Mark 14:61-64

other details—betrayal by a friend (41:9); vinegar offered for His thirst (69:21); prayer committing spirit to Father (31:5); no bones broken (34:20); resurrection from the dead (16:10).

Isaiah, sometimes called the gospel prophet, beautifully and clearly pictured the coming Messiah. Eight centuries before the coming of the Messiah he predicted: He would be born of a virgin and would be called Immanuel which means "God with us" (7:14); be of the family of Jesse (11:1); the Spirit of the Lord would be on Him (11:2). He would minister in Galilee (9:1); would be judge (33:22); a voice in the wilderness would prepare the way (40:3). The fifty-third chapter of Isaiah contains many messianic references: He would be rejected by His own people (53:3); be physically wounded and bruised and spit upon (53:5-6); did not answer His accusers (53:7); killed with thieves yet interceded for the transgressors (53:12); He was buried in a rich man's tomb (53:9).

About 750 B.C. Micah wrote, "But you, O Bethlehem Ephrathah, who are little to be among the clans of Judah, from you shall come forth for me one who is to be ruler in Israel, whose origin is from old, from ancient days" (Micah 5:2). From this passage, the Jewish scholars were able to inform the wise men that the Messiah was to be born in Bethlehem (Matthew 2:4-6). The birth of Jesus in Bethlehem is another evidence that He was their promised One of God.

Daniel foresaw a coming "Son of Man" (Daniel 7:13). This was Jesus' favorite title as He identified Himself as the promised Messiah. In the synagogue in His home town of Nazareth, Jesus read from Isaiah 61 and then declared, "Today this scripture has been fulfilled in your hearing" (Luke 4:21). The local carpenter (Mark 6:3) then said, "Isaiah was talking about me!" Christ's fulfillment of Old Testament prophecy is a strong evidence that He is the Son of God.

Miracles

The miracles that Jesus worked provide further evidence of His deity. Nicodemus, a ruler of the Jews who came to

MIRACLES

A *miracle* is an event in the external world worked by the direct power of God intended as a sign.

New Testament Words for Miracles:
Works — emphasize the power involved
Signs — emphasize the purpose of miracles
Wonders — emphasize the effect on observers

Miracles as Credentials (Demonstrations of Divine Authority):
Matthew 9:6-7; 11:21-23; Mark 2:10; Luke 7:22; John 5:36; 10:24-25; 10:37-38; 14:10-11; 15:24; 20:31; Acts 2:22; Hebrews 2:3-4.

Jesus by night, said to Jesus, "We know that you are a teacher come from God; for no one can do these signs that you do unless God is with him" (John 3:2).

Four friends brought a paralyzed man to Jesus to be healed. Because of the crowd they could not get into the room where Jesus was. They took the man up on the roof and removed some tiles. They lowered the paralytic on a pallet to Jesus in the room below. Jesus announced to the man, "Your sins are forgiven." The scribes thought Jesus was a blasphemer for such a statement. How could one know? The man did not suddenly turn white as snow so everyone could tell his sins had been forgiven. He still looked the same. Jesus asked them which was easier — to forgive his sins or to heal him instantly. Then Jesus said, "That you may know that the Son of Man has authority on earth to forgive sins," he said to the paralytic, "I say to you, rise, take up your pallet and go home" (Mark 2:10). Jesus used physical miracles, visible to the senses, to demonstrate His spiritual authority.

THE MIRACLES OF JESUS

Power over Nature

1) The water changed into wine – John 2:1-11
2) The first miraculous catch of fish – Luke 5:1-7
3) The stilling of the storm on the Sea of Galilee –
   Matthew 8:23-27; Mark 4:36-41; Luke 8:22-25
4) Feeding of 5000 from lad's lunch – Matthew 14:15-21;
   Mark 6:30-34; Luke 9:10-17; John 6:1-14
5) Walking on Sea of Galilee – Matthew 14:22-32; Mark 6:45-46;
   John 6:15-21
6) The feeding of the 4000 – Matthew 15:32-39;
   Mark 8:1-9
7) Finding the tribute money in the fish's mouth –
   Matthew 17:24-27
8) Cursing of the fig tree – Matthew 21:18-22;
   Mark 11:12-14, 20-24
9) The second miraculous catch of fish – John 21:1-11

Power to Heal Diseases

1) The healing of the nobleman's son at Capernaum –
   John 4:46-54
2) Peter's wife's mother healed of a fever – Matthew 8:14-18;
   Mark 1:29-34; Luke 4:38-41
3) The first cleansing of a leper – Matthew 8:1-4; Mark 1:40-45;
   Luke 5:12-14
4) The healing of a paralyzed man – Matthew 9:1-8; Mark 2:3-12;
   Luke 5:18-26
5) The healing of the lame man at the Pool of Bethesda –
   John 5:1-16
6) The man with the withered hand – Matthew 12:9-14; Mark 3:1-6;
   Luke 6:6-11
7) The paralyzed centurion's servant – Matthew 8:5-13; Luke 7:1-10
8) The woman with the issue of blood – Matthew 9:20-22;
   Mark 5:25-34; Luke 8:43-48

9) The restoring of sight to two blind men — Matthew 9:27-31
10) The healing of the deaf and mute man — Matthew 15:29-31; Mark 7:31-37
11) The restoration of sight to the blind man outside of Bethesda — Mark 8:22-26
12) The cleansing of ten lepers — Luke 17:11-19
13) The man born blind — John 9
14) The woman with the bent back — Luke 13:10-17
15) The man with dropsy — Luke 14:1-6
16) The two blind men near Jericho — Matthew 20:29-34; Mark 10:46-52
17) The restoration of the severed ear to Malchus — Luke 22:50-51

Casting Demons out of Persons

1) The man with an unclean spirit in the synagogue at Capernaum — Mark 1:23-28; Luke 4:33-37
2) The man who was both blind and mute — Matthew 12:22-30; Mark 3:22-30; Luke 11:14-23
3) Two possessed with demons at Gadara — Matthew 8:28-34; Mark 5:1-21; Luke 8:26-40
4) A mute man — Matthew 9:32-34
5) The daughter of the Syrophoenician woman — Matthew 15:21-28; Mark 7:24-30
6) The child, after the Transfiguration — Matthew 17:14-21; Mark 9:14-29; Luke 9:37-43

Resurrections from the Dead

1) The son of the widow of Nain — Luke 7:11-18
2) The daughter of Jairus — Matthew 9:18-19,23-26; Mark 5:21-24,35-43; Luke 8:40-42,49-56
3) Lazarus — John 11
4) His own resurrection — Matthew 28; Mark 16; Luke 24; John 20-21

On a grassy slope on the northeast corner of the Sea of Galilee, Jesus miraculously fed 5,000 men plus women and children from a lad's lunch (John 6:1-14). This lunch — five flat, hard rolls and two small fish — was miraculously multiplied to provide a smorgasbord dinner for the crowd. The disciples even gathered up twelve baskets of leftovers.

Jesus' words, "Peace be still," quieted not only the stormy wind but also the tempestuous waves on the Sea of Galilee. Jesus walked on the water of the Sea of Galilee. Some reject this miracle saying He would have had to destroy the law of gravity. Did the boat float to heaven? No! He did not destroy the gravitational force. When a ball is thrown into the air, the law of gravity is not broken. A greater power than the pull of gravity is introduced. Jesus demonstrated a power greater than the normal pull of gravity. The God who caused nature to behave in a normal way could cause it to behave in an unusual way for His special purpose.

After the disciples experienced a night of futile fishing, Jesus told them to put the nets on the other side. The result was a miraculous catch of fish. Jesus demonstrated not only power over the elements but also He healed all manner of sickness, diseases, and physical deformities.

He healed a man who was born blind. Neighbors brought the healed man to the Pharisees who questioned him about his healing. They even quizzed his parents who confirmed that the man was their son and had been born blind. As to his healing they said, "Ask him; he is of age" (John 9:21). The Jewish leaders insisted Jesus was a sinner because He worked on the Sabbath. In the face of repeated cross examination, the healed man insisted, "One thing I know, that though I was blind, now I see" (John 9:25). They could not refute his testimony.

Jesus showed His supernatural power by raising the daughter of Jairus and the son of the widow of Nain from the dead. As Jesus approached the tomb of Lazarus, practical Martha said, "Lord, by this time there will be an odor, for he has been dead four days" (John 11:39). Jesus had the stone removed from the door of the tomb. He then prayed and called "Lazarus, come out" (John 11:43). One has quipped, "If Jesus had not named Lazarus, He would have emptied all the graves!" Jesus had that kind of power. Lazarus walked out of his tomb. This awesome miracle did not just return the spirit to the body but also reconstituted all the cells of the body to a living condition.

When Jesus claimed equality with the Father, the Jews wanted to stone him. Jesus cited his works as a credential for His claims. "If I am not doing the works of my father, then do not believe me; but if I do them, even though you do not believe me, believe the works, that you may know and understand that the Father is in me, and I am in the Father" (John 10:37-38). Jesus did not demand blind allegiance. He appealed to His miracles as reasonable evidence for accepting His deity.

Resurrection

The resurrection is a convincing credential verifying that Jesus stands true as the Son of God. The crucial question relating to the truth of Christianity is — "Did Jesus actually rise from the dead!" If He did, then Christianity stands true. If He did not, then it is sheer foolishness. Paul, the former enemy of Christ, underscores the importance of the resurrection. "If Christ has not been raised, your faith is futile and you are still in your sins" (1 Corinthians 15:17).

If Christ were not raised from the dead, these consequences would be true:
1) Jesus would not be the Son of God;
2) Christianity would not be the true religion;
3) The gospel message would be false;
4) No salvation or hope could be found in Christ.

The seriousness of these consequences makes it imperative that we consider the evidence for the resurrection.

Paul affirms, "But in fact Christ has been raised from the dead" (1 Corinthians 15:20). The evidence that Christ is risen may be summarized under these headings: the empty tomb, His personal appearances, and the historical results.

The Empty Tomb

Jesus was buried in a tomb with a heavy circular stone that moved in a channel at the door. Knowing Jesus' promise to rise again, His enemies received permission from Pilate to put a guard of soldiers at the door of the grave. The guards at the tomb and the seal around the stone guaranteed that the disciples did not steal the body. The guards reported the resurrection to the chief priests, who bribed them to tell the lie that the disciples stole the body while they were asleep (Matthew 28:11-15).

The women who went to anoint the body of Jesus found the tomb empty. The angel announced to them, "He is not here; for He has risen" (Matthew 28:6). The disciples doubted the report of the women. Peter and John had to go see for themselves. Like the proverbial Missourian — they had to be shown. They were not naive and gullible men who believed six miracles before breakfast every morning. They were everyday people who insisted on the facts. None of the disciples (with the possible exception of John, see John 20:8-9) were convinced that Jesus was alive again merely from the evidence of the empty tomb.

Just north of the city wall of Jerusalem near Gordon's Calvary is a Garden Tomb that some hold to be the very tomb where Jesus was buried. We cannot be positive that this is the tomb of Jesus. But we *can* be positive that His tomb was empty.

The Greek text implies that the grave clothes seen by the women and the disciples in the tomb were in the same shape they had been when wrapped around the body.[2] This cocoon-shape of the wrappings indicated a miraculous disappearance of the body and not a grave robbery.

His Personal Appearances

It took the bodily appearances of the risen Jesus to convince the disciples that Jesus was alive from the dead. Some have rejected the appearances as hallucinations. No evidence exists of delusion on the part of the witnesses. What one saw they all saw. Psychologically, they were not programmed for dreaming up the idea of the resurrection. If the appearances were not real, why didn't the enemies produce the dead body to quiet the Christians' claims?

In the garden Jesus appeared first to Mary Magdalene and then to the other women. Jesus appeared after His resurrection at least ten times. He appeared to individuals, to groups and once to more than five hundred people (1 Corinthians 15:5-8). Paul reminds his readers most of these 500 are still alive, implying they could check with the witnesses themselves if they desired. In and near Jerusalem He appeared in the garden, on a roadway, in an upper room and on the Mt. of Olives. He also appeared on a mountain and by the seaside in Galilee. The disciples were not expecting the resurrection for they considered the testimony of the women as "an idle tale, and they did not believe them" (Luke 24:11).

The two on the road to Emmaus expressed their disappointment in these words, "We had hoped that he was the one to restore Israel" (Luke 24:21). When they recognized Jesus, they raced the seven miles back into Jerusalem to tell the other disciples.

On the evening of Resurrection Day, Jesus appeared to the ten apostles in an upper room. Thomas, who was not present, insisted that he would not believe until he saw for himself. Because of this one incident he is often called "Doubting Thomas." A week later Jesus appeared to the eleven in the upper room. He called Thomas to see His wounds and said, "Do not be faithless, but believing" (John 20:27). Thomas responded, "My Lord and my God" (John 20:28).

Perhaps it is good that the disciples were all doubters. They were honest and stubborn — unwilling to accept something unless forced by the facts. A. B. Bruce well said, "The evangelists have carefully chronicled these doubts that all might have no doubt."[3]

Christ appeared to Saul of Tarsus on the road to Damascus where Saul planned to imprison Christians. It took the bodily appearance of the risen Jesus to change this strong-willed Jew from being an unbeliever in Christ and a killer of Christians to total commitment to Jesus as the divine Lord of his life.

The apostles boldly proclaimed the unpopular message throughout the Roman empire that Jesus had risen from the dead. Beatings, prison and even death did not cause them to renounce their testimony. Charles Colson who was involved in the Watergate scandal said that this incident was one thing that convinced him of the truth of the resurrection. He said that those involved — Ehrlichman, Haldeman, Mitchell, and himself — all believed in President Nixon and had great power at their fingertips.

> Yet even at the prospect of jeopardizing the President, even in the face of all the privileges of the most powerful office in the world, the threat of embarassment, perhaps jail, was so overpowering and the instinct for self-preservation so over-whelming, that one by one, those involved deserted their leader to save their own skin.
>
> What has that got to do with the resurrection? Simply this: Watergate demonstrates human nature. No one can ever make me believe that eleven ordinary human beings would for 40 years endure persecution, beatings, prison, and death, without ever once renouncing that Jesus Christ was risen from the dead.[4]

"And with great power the apostles gave their testimony to the resurrection of the Lord Jesus" (Acts 4:33).

The Historical Results

Many historical results cannot be explained apart from the fact of the resurrection. Only the resurrection explains the transformation in character of denying Peter, unbelieving half-brother James, and persecuting Saul. Only the fact of the resurrection made possible the resurrection faith which accounts for the origin and growth of the church. Conscience and honesty led a great many of the priests to be "obedient to the faith" (Acts 6:7). Early Christian writers tell us that the

POST-RESURRECTION APPEARANCES OF JESUS

1) Women returning from tomb — Matthew 28:1-10
2) Mary Magdalene at the tomb — Mark 16:9-11; John 20:11-18
3) Peter — Luke 24:34; 1 Corinthians 15:5
4) Cleopas and another disciple — Mark 16:12; Luke 24:13-35
5) Ten apostles (Thomas absent) — Mark 16:14-18; Luke 24:36-40; John 20:19-23; 1 Corinthians 15:5
6) Eleven apostles (Thomas present) — John 20:26-28
7) Disciples at Sea of Galilee — John 21:1-23
8) Apostles, above 500 brethren, on mountain in Galilee — Matthew 28:16-20; 1 Corinthians 15:6
9) James — 1 Corinthians 15:7
10) Apostles on Mount of Olives before ascension — Mark 16:19; Luke 24:50-52; Acts 1:3-8

Christians worshiped on the first day because this was the day Christ arose.[5] The validity of baptism is linked to the resurrection (Romans 6:4-6; Colossians 2:12-13; 1 Peter 3:21). The Lord's Supper is not just remembering a dead martyr but is communion with a living Lord.

What does the resurrection of Christ mean? It means that the living God of the universe has acted in history. God is real. Christ is Lord, God in flesh. Man has hope through Christ. Michael Green, a British writer, tells this story:

> I remember a research scientist once saying to me that he thought the story of Jesus mythical. I asked him when he had last read it. He had to admit it was a very long time ago. I said to him something like this: 'You are a scientist. You are accustomed to modifying your preconceived theories if the evidence warrants it. I suggest that you apply the same principle here. Examine the evidence at first hand. Be open to where it may lead you. Just follow the truth, and see what happens.'[6]

Mr. Green met that man some months later at a Christian meeting. "I did what you suggested," he said, "and it has brought me into the Christian camp."[7]

It is imperative that we challenge everyone to consider the claims and credentials of Christ. At closing time as people were leaving an exhibit of Rembrandt's paintings, a few made derogatory comments about the artist and his work. A custodian remarked to them, "It is not the artist but the viewers who are on trial."

This chapter has examined the identity of Jesus. But actually those who look at Jesus are the ones on trial. The case rests. Each must make his or her choice. The evidence shows that Jesus is the Son of God and the Savior of man.

The scene of Christ dying a painful, shameful death on the cross looked like a defeat — a bright, young leader cut down in the flower of His youth. France was led by Napoleon in a war against England led by Wellington. In 1815 the decisive battle was fought. A messenger reported the result of the battle by giving flag signals across the English Channel to London. The message read, "Wellington defeated." The fog closed in and the people could not see the rest of the message. They assumed England had lost. London felt the sting of defeat. But when the fog lifted, they learned the completed message, "Wellington defeated the enemy."

The cross looked like Christ defeated. But on the third day He rose from the dead completing the message, "Christ defeated the enemy." On Friday the world said, "No," to God. But on that resurrection Sunday God said, "Yes," to the world. *Jesus Stands True as the Son of God.*

"Scripture cannot be broken." *John 10:35*

"Thy word is truth." *John 17:17*

"All scripture is inspired by God." *2 Timothy 3:16*

"No prophecy ever came by the impulse of man, but men moved by the Holy Spirit spoke from God." *2 Peter 1:21*

"And we also thank God constantly for this, that when you received the word of God which you heard from us, you accepted it not as the word of men but as what it really is, the word of God." *1 Thessalonians 2:13*

"The basic question about the inspiration and authority of Scripture is 'What do you think of Christ?' If we accept Him as Lord, it is consitent to submit to His teaching on the complete authority of Scripture." *Kenneth Kantzer*

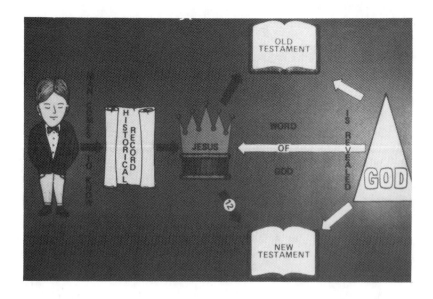

Chapter Five

THE BIBLE STANDS TRUE AS THE WORD OF GOD

A CASE FOR THE INSPIRATION OF THE BIBLE

1) The New Testament books meet the tests of reliable history.

2) Reliable New Testament records state that Jesus of Nazareth claimed to be God in the flesh.

3) Supernatural credentials of fulfilled prophecy, miracles, and His resurrection verify Jesus' claims to deity.

4) As God, all Jesus taught is true and authoritative.

5) Jesus taught that the Old Testament was a true Word from God and promised Holy Spirit inspiration which resulted in the New Testament.

6) The Bible is the Word of God.

PART 1 — INSPIRATION CLAIMED

A young Bible college student wrote these statements about the Bible:

Either the Bible is the Word of God or it is not.
If the Bible is the Word of God and I do not
follow it, then I am a fool.

If the Bible is not the Word of God and I do
follow it, then I am a fool.
I must decide — Is the Bible the true Word of God?

QUESTIONS WE CANNOT ANSWER
WITHOUT A WORD FROM GOD

1) How can my sin be forgiven?
2) Who am I?
3) How should I live?
4) Is there life after death?

We must answer the question, "Is the Bible the true Word
from God?"

A word from God is needed to resolve many issues. A
word from God is necessary in order to answer the question,
"How can our sins be forgiven?" Reason, feelings, and experience cannot infallibly assure us that our sins are forgiven.
Since sin is ultimately against God, forgiveness of sins must
be based upon what He says.

To answer the questions, "Who am I?" and "How should I
live?" we need a word from God. Many brilliant thinkers of
our day do not know the answers to these questions because
they do not know God and do not accept His word. If God
made man, then man needs a message from God to know
who man is and how he should live.

"Is there life after death?" Plato in his dialogue on immortality, *Phaedo*, admits that though we can reason about life
after death, "We can never know for sure unless we have
some sure word from God."[1]

The testimonials of life-after-death experiences are ambigu-
ous. Neither reason nor experience can prove life after death.
The answer awaits a word from God.

Is the Bible the true Word from God? Mere claims to inspiration do not prove that a book is in fact the Word of God. Many books make false claims. How can we establish that the Bible is the Word of God without assuming the conclusion?

Evidence demonstrates that the New Testament stands true as history. From this reliable historical record it is clear that Jesus of Nazareth made claims to deity. His claims to be equal with God were supported by His divine credentials. Jesus stands true as the Son of God.

If Jesus is God-come-to-earth, then what He says on any topic is true. What Jesus says about the origin and authority of the Bible is the truth. He held the Old Testament to be the Word of God. He promised the apostles Holy Spirit inspiration, which then provided the New Testament. Before examining Jesus' testimony about the Bible in the next chapter, this chapter will seek to investigate what kind of inspiration the Bible claims for itself.

What is meant by the term "inspiration of the Bible?" Does the Bible in fact claim to be the inspired Word of God? What are some ways people have misunderstood inspiration? Have Christians through the centuries affirmed the inspiration of the Bible? How should we answer the challenges to the authority of the Bible?

Inspiration Defined

Inspiration means that God guided the writers by the Holy Spirit so they wrote the truth He wanted written without error or omission of necessary truth. Does this definition square with the Bible's claims for itself?

DEFINITIONS

Revelation   Communication of His nature and will from God to man

General revelation Disclosure of God's truth in nature

Special revelation Disclosure of God's truth in Scripture and in Christ

Inspiration   God guided the writers by the Holy Spirit so that they wrote the truth He wanted written without error or omission of necessary truth

Inerrancy   The original Scriptures were characterized by complete truthfulness, having no error (Infallible)

Authority   The right to command obedience

Canon   List of inspired books

Inspiration Claimed

In honestly investigating a book we must first understand clearly what the book claims for itself. We must not claim more or less for the Bible's inspiration than it claims for itself. Paul declares, "All scripture is inspired by God" (2 Timothy 3:16). God produced the Scripture through prophets and apostles. Peter stated, "No prophecy ever came by the impulse of man, but men moved by the Holy Spirit spoke from God" (2 Peter 1:21).

Biblical writers claimed they received their message from God. The phrase "thus says the Lord" or its equivalent occurs nearly 4,000 times in the Old Testament.

The books written by Moses are filled with claims of inspiration. In Exodus we read, "Moses came and told the people all the words of the Lord and all the ordinances . . . and Moses wrote all the words of the Lord" (Exodus 24:3-4). After the return from Babylonian captivity, Ezra and Nehemiah affirmed that the Law of Moses was given by God (Ezra 9:4; Nehemiah 8:2).

In Psalm 119 David calls the Scriptures "the word [or words] of the Lord" twenty-four times. David said, "The Spirit of the LORD speaks by me, his word is upon my tongue" (2 Samuel 23:2).

The seventeen books of prophecy in the Old Testament contain hundreds of expressions such as, "Hear the word of the LORD," "the mouth of the LORD hath spoken," "thus the LORD said unto me." Such expressions are found 120 times in Isaiah, 430 in Jeremiah, and 329 times in Ezekiel. All of the last twelve prophets begin their books with the words, "The word of the LORD came to . . . ." To Jeremiah God said, "I have put my words in your mouth" (Jeremiah 1:9). To Ezekiel He said, "You shall speak my words to them" (Ezekiel 2:7).

In the New Testament Scriptures we also read claims by Christ and the apostles that they declared the Word of God. Jesus said, "I have not spoken on my own authority; the Father who sent me has himself given me commandment what to say and what to speak" (John 12:49). The preaching of Jesus was called the "word of God" (Luke 5:1).

Paul told the Thessalonians that the message he preached to them was "the word of God" (1 Thessalonians 2:13). Frequently in the book of Acts Luke called the apostles' preaching "the word of God" (Acts 8:14; 11:1; 12:24; 13:7, 44; 15:35; 17:13; 18:11; 19:20). Paul wrote to the Galatians, "The gospel which was preached by me is not man's gospel. For I did not receive it from man, nor was I taught it, but it came through a revelation of Jesus Christ" (Galatians 1:11-12). Paul claimed the apostles received a revelation from the Spirit of God (1 Corinthians 2:6-12). "And we impart this in words not taught by human wisdom but taught by the Spirit" (1 Corinthains 2:13). Paul claimed a divine authority for his letters. He told the Thessalonians that if they rejected his letter, they rejected "not man but God" (1 Thessalonians 4:8).

Inspiration Clarified

Three clarifications are helpful in understanding the Bible's claims to inspiration.

Inspiration does not mean that the Holy Spirit dictated word for word to the writers. The Bible writers were not made into automatic transcription machines. God allowed the writers to use their own personal vocabulary and style in expressing the truth he wanted communicated. He did keep them from falsehood.

Inspiration does not imply literalism. The Bible uses figurative expressions as does most every form of communication. A skeptical college professor liked to ask students entering his class, "Is there anyone in this class so foolish as to believe in the literal truth of the whole Bible?" If some dared to raise hands, he would then ask, "When our Lord told his followers to 'go tell Herod that fox,' do you believe that Herod was a four-footed, furry animal? Obviously not, therefore you do not believe in the literal truth of the New Testament."

Then he would test them on the Old Testament, "The Psalmist declares that 'the hills clap their hands for joy.' Do you believe that the Judean hills slammed themselves together out of sheer joy? Of course not. You do not believe in the literal truth of the Old Testament either."[2] No verse in the Old Testament says hills clap their hands. Perhaps the professor was thinking of Psalm 98:8, "Let the floods clap their hands: let the hills sing for joy together."

The Bible uses figurative language to express truth even as in common conversation people talk about the sunset or say,

"He is fast as lightning." We understand God's truth when we understand the Bible author's *intended meaning*. Some fear stressing the inspiration and authority of the Bible will result in a superstitious worship of the book itself. But cherishing and rereading a love letter does not mean one worships the letter. The letter is appreciated because it is a message from a loved one. Christians do not worship the book but respect and obey the message in the Bible because they trust and honor God who gave His word to man.

INSPIRATION

Does Not Mean:	**Does Mean:**
Mechanical Dictation	The writers used their own style of writing
Literalism	The writers used figurative expressions as well as literal to express truth
Bible Worship	The Bible itself is not to be worshiped but its message is to be obeyed

---

Inspiration Affirmed

The inspiration of the Bible has been affirmed both by the Jews of Jesus' day and by Christians through the centuries. The Jews of Jesus' day held the Old Testament to be the Word of God. Josephus, a Jewish historian writing about A.D. 90, represents this view. Of the Old Testament he stated, ". . . nor is there any disagreement in what is written." The prophets have written "of things as they learned them of God himself by inspiration."[3] Throughout the centuries, Christians have accepted the inspiration of the Bible. In the first Christian writing outside the New Testament (A.D. 96), Clement of Rome wrote, "Look carefully into the scriptures, which are the true utterances of the Holy Spirit."[4] Justin Martyr said of the utterances of the prophets, "You must not suppose that they were spoken by the inspired themselves, but by the Divine word who moves them."[5] "I am entirely convinced that no Scripture contradicts another."[6]

Irenaeus in A.D. 180 wrote, "The Scriptures are indeed perfect, since they were spoken by the Word of God and His Spirit."[7] Augustine in a letter to Jerome written in A.D. 405 affirmed, "I have learned to yield this respect and honor only to the canonical books of Scripture, of these alone do I most firmly believe that the authors were completely free from error."[8] Thomas Aquinas, in the thirteenth century said, "The author of holy Scripture is God."[9]

Martin Luther, the sixteenth century reformer, said, "The Scriptures have never erred."[10] "The Scriptures cannot err."[11] John Calvin stated of the Bible, "God is . . . its author." He affirmed, "We owe the Scripture the same reverence we owe God, since it has its only source in Him."[12] Calvin referred to the Bible as "The infallible rule of his holy truth."[13]

**EARLY TESTIMONY
TO INSPIRATION AND
INERRANCY OF THE BIBLE**

Josephus	AD 90
Clement of Rome	AD 96
Justin Martyr	AD 140
Irenaeus	AD 180
Augustine	AD 405

Inspiration Challenged

The authority and inspiration of the Bible have been challenged on both the practical and intellectual levels. What are the challenges?

Several years ago this writer was preaching in a small midwestern church. In a conversation after Sunday dinner a lady emphasized that the church is "of the people, by the people, and for the people." She had no Bible reference to document her statement. Many have the mistaken idea that the church is a democracy where a majority vote rules on what is believed and practiced. But the New Testament pictures the church as a kingdom. The authority of the King must be obeyed.

A fine Christian gentleman who knew the Bible well gave a young preacher some valuable advice, "You need to preach that the church is a kingdom. We need to stress the authority of the King. The Bible is the word of our King."

However, not everyone accepts the Bible as true. A Christian high school boy who had a New Testament in his pocket was asked by another student, "What's that book of fairy tales?"

An African Christian, who had been a cannibal, was reading his Bible. A European businessman came up to him and asked, "What's that book you are reading?"

The converted cannibal answered, "I am reading my Bible."

The European man looked down his nose condescendingly and replied, "Well, that book is out of date back in my country."

The African did not smile. He pointed over to a large pot of boiling water and said, "Do you see that pot of boiling water?"

The man apprehensively said, "Well, yes."

The African said, "If this book were out of date in my country, you'd be in that pot right now." It *does* make a difference whether or not one believes the Bible.

At college a Christian young man found his faith in the Bible under attack. He said, "At home people believe the

Bible is true from cover to cover, but here at college they give me reasons why I can't believe in the Bible. My church never gave me good reasons for believing the Bible. So if I am honest, I will have to give up my trust in the Bible." But the critics can be answered. There are good reasons for believing in the Bible.

Skeptics have always been ready to attack the Bible. Voltaire, French unbeliever, said it took twelve men to write up Christianity and he would show how Christianity could be destroyed. But within one hundred years, Bibles were being published in the very building where he wrote this statement.

In the earliest years of the church the apostles' word was the final authority in the church. Then councils arose in which a few church leaders made decisions that many held to be authoritative for the entire church. Eventually the time came when some invested the authority of the church in a single individual, the pope of Rome.

In the 1500s men like Martin Luther protested, contending that it was not right to be bound by human authorities and human traditions. Luther insisted, "Let our conscience be bound only by the Word of God. The Word of God must be our only final authority." The reformers made a valiant effort to restore the Bible to its rightful place of authority.

In the last few centuries many have made human thinking their highest authority. The highest authority for some was science, for others, philosophy, and for still others, theology. Lewis Foster was a student at Yale Divinity School. He asked Dean Luther Weigle, "What is your highest authority?"

Dr. Weigle pointed to his temple and responded, "Right in here." He candidly admitted his own thinking was his highest authority.

Those claiming to be Christian have three primary choices for a final authority—the Bible, the church, or man. For many the Bible is not the final authority. Some look to church tradition, denominational creeds, and literature, and church officials as their authority. Even the statement, "I know the Bible says that, but we have never done it that way" expresses a form of church authority. When the plain meaning of

Scripture is not accepted because we think or feel differently, we have chosen a human authority.

```
┌─────────────────────────────┐
│                             │
│          HIGHEST            │
│         AUTHORITY?          │
│                             │
│           Bible?            │
│                             │
│           Church?           │
│                             │
│            Man?             │
│                             │
└─────────────────────────────┘
```

How can we decide if the Bible, the church, or human thinking is to be our highest authority? What reason would convince an honest seeker to accept the Bible's claims to divine inspiration? This study did not begin by assuming that the Bible is the Word of God. Strong evidence shows that the New Testament stands true as history. Jesus of Nazareth claimed to be God-in-flesh. His resurrection and other credentials establish His deity. We can trust what Jesus taught on any subject is the final truth on that subject.

The next chapter will state what Jesus taught about the Old Testament and what He promised about the New Testament. If Jesus taught that the Bible is the inspired Word of God, then we have the strongest reason for believing that *the Bible Stands True as the Word of God.*

Jesus promised Holy Spirit inspiration to the apostles.

The Gospel writers recorded the life of
Christ within 20 to 60 years after His ascension.

Chapter Six
THE BIBLE STANDS TRUE AS THE WORD OF GOD

PART 2 — INSPIRATION CONFIRMED

The last chapter stated the Bible's claims to inspiration. This chapter will present Jesus' teaching that the Bible is the Word of God.

The Bible throughout makes thousands of claims that it is expressing the word of the God of this universe. Either these claims are true or they are false! Those who do not believe these claims have an obligation at least to check them out to see if they are true or not. If these claims are false, then they should be rejected. They would not be innocent mistakes but outrageous misrepresentations. Convincing evidence, however, supports the Bible's claim to be inspired by God.

Various lines of evidence could be presented to support the Bible's claim to be the Word of God — Jesus' teaching concerning Scripture, the fulfillment of prophecy, and the argument from experience. Although a study of each of these would be profitable, this chapter will state Jesus' teaching concerning Scripture, which is the strongest case for believing the Bible's inspiration.

The New Testament stands true as history. Jesus stands true as the Son of God. As the Son of God, He is our highest authority for any subject about which He taught. If Jesus teaches that the Bible is in fact the Word of God, then we can know that it is so.

Jesus' Teaching About the Old Testament

First, we will investigate what Jesus said about the Old

Testament and then what He said about the New Testament. What did Jesus, the Son of God, teach about the Old Testament? What Jesus believed and taught about the Old Testament is what a Christian wants to believe. Jesus said that the Old Testament is true, inspired, authoritative, and prophetic.

Historically True

Jesus accepted the Old Testament as historically true. This writer has asked many groups of people what stories are rejected today by those who do not believe the Old Testament. The answers include the creation, the flood, Jonah and the whale, as well as others. It is significant that the events in the Old Testament most often rejected today were clearly accepted by Jesus in His teaching.

If Jesus, the Son of God, accepted the Genesis creation account, then Christians also should accept it. Jesus said to the Pharisees, "Have you not read that he who made them from the beginning made them male and female, and said, 'For this reason a man shall leave his father and mother and be joined to his wife, and the two shall become one flesh.'" (Matthew 19:4-5). Obviously he referred to the Genesis record of the creation because He quoted from Genesis 2:24 as an authoritative statement about marriage made by God Himself at the time of creation.

Today many scoff at the idea of a global flood but several times Jesus referred to Noah and the flood as a historical fact (Matthew 24:37-39; Luke 17:26-27). Some have a hard time swallowing the story of Jonah and the whale. Jesus had no reservations about accepting this event. He used it as an illustration and prediction of His resurrection from the dead (Matthew 12:38-40). Jesus referred to the incident of Moses at the burning bush (Mark 12:26). Jesus said Naaman the Syrian was cleansed of leprosy in the days of Elisha (Luke 4:27). Jesus mentioned that God sent Elijah to the widow of Zarephath for whom food was miraculously provided (Luke

4:25). Jesus also mentioned Lot's wife (Luke 17:32), those healed from snakebites who looked on the brass serpent (John 3:14) and other events. Everywhere in His teaching Jesus treated the Old Testament as a historically true record.

Critics have denied the authorship of many Old Testament books, especially those traditionally held to be written by Moses, Isaiah, and Daniel. Jesus spoke of the book of Moses in citing the event of the burning bush (Exodus 3:6; Mark 12:26). In quoting from Exodus, Leviticus, and Deuteronomy, Jesus cited Moses as the author (Exodus 20:12; 21:17; Deuteronomy 5:16; Leviticus 20:9; Mark 7:10). Twice Jesus referred to Isaiah as the author of statements quoted from the book of Isaiah (Isaiah 6:9-10; Matthew 13:14; 15:7). He identified Daniel as the author of a statement from Daniel 9:27 (Matthew 24:15).

JESUS ACCEPTED THE
OLD TESTAMENT AS HISTORICALLY TRUE

Miraculous Events Often Rejected Today, Accepted by Jesus

Creation of man and woman — Matthew 19:4-5
Noah and the flood — Matthew 24:37-39; Luke 17:26-27
Jonah swallowed by great fish — Matthew 12:38-40
Burning bush — Mark 12:26
Naaman cleansed of leprosy in Jordan River —Luke 4:27
Miraculous food supply for widow of Zarephath —Luke 4:25
Lot's wife becoming a pillar of salt —Luke 17:32
People healed by looking on brass serpent —John 3:14

Authorship of Old Testament Books
Often Denied Today, Accepted by Jesus

Moses	Mark 12:26 (Exodus 3:6); Mark 7:10 (Exodus 20:12; 21:17; Deuteronomy 5:16; Leviticus 20:9)
Isaiah	Matthew 13:14; 15:7 (Isaiah 6:9-10)
Daniel	Matthew 24:15 (Daniel 9:27)

Inspired by God

Jesus also taught that the Old Testament was inspired by God. In a conversation with some Sadducees, Jesus said, "Have you not read what was said to you by God, 'I am the God of Abraham, and the God of Isaac and the God of Jacob'" (Matthew 22:31-32). What Moses wrote was also said by God.

To the Pharisees Jesus said, "You have a fine way of rejecting the commandment of God, in order to keep your tradition! For Moses said, 'Honor your father and your mother'" (Mark 7:9-10). After Christ showed how they denied the real meaning of the Old Testament, He commented that they were "thus making void the word of God" (Mark 7:13).

Some think David was inspired by the beauty of the stars and the sheep on the hillside to write the poetry of the Psalms. But Jesus affirmed a higher source for his inspiration, "David himself, inspired by the Holy Spirit, declared. . ." (Mark 12:36). In a defense of His deity Jesus referred to the authority and total trustworthiness of Scripture, "Scripture cannot be broken" (John 10:35). One can have complete confidence in Scripture because it is God's word. It will not prove false.

JESUS AFFIRMED
INSPIRATION OF THE OLD TESTAMENT

He cited Old Testament statements as:

"Said to you by God" — Matthew 22:31

"Commandments of God" — Mark 7:9

"The word of God" — Mark 7:13

"Inspired by the Holy Spirit" — Mark 12:36

"Scripture cannot be broken" — John 10:35

Divine Authority

Jesus accepted the Old Testament as historically true, inspired by God, and as having divine authority. Jesus did not come with a burn-your-Old-Testament approach. He said to trust the Scripture because it bears the authority of God.

To the Jews our Lord said, "You search the Scriptures because you think that in them you have eternal life; and it is they that bear witness to me" (John 5:39). You are looking in the right place but you do not have enough confidence in your book. "If you believed Moses, you would believe me, for he wrote of me. But if you do not believe his writings, how will you believe my words?" (John 5:46-47). If the Jews would have accepted the truth and authority of the Old Testament, then they naturally would have accepted the claims of Jesus, the promised Messiah.

In Jesus' teaching about the rich man and Lazarus, the rich man in torment asked that Lazarus be sent back to earth to warn his brothers. "But Abraham said, 'they have Moses and the prophets; let them hear them.' And he said, 'No, father Abraham; but if some one goes to them from the dead, they will repent.' He said to him, 'If they do not hear Moses and the prophets, neither will they be convinced if someone should rise from the dead'" (Luke 16:29-31). This shows Jesus' respect for the authority of the Old Testament.

When Jesus was tempted by the devil, He did not say, "I've been reading a good article in a psychology magazine and it says . . . ." To each temptation Jesus quoted Scripture. "It is written" was equal to "God says." Jesus relied on the Word of God with absolute trust and obedience. Jesus appealed to the Old Testament to settle arguments with the Jews (Matthew 12:3, 4-5, 7; 21:16; 22:32, 44). He chided the Jews for taking the Old Testament lightly (Matthew 19:4-5; 21:16, 42; 22:31-32; Mark 12:26). He often asked, "Have you not read this Scripture?" (Mark 12:10; Matthew 21:16, 42). He told the Sadducees, "You are wrong, because you know neither the scriptures nor the power of God" (Matthew 22:29). Jesus taught that the Old Testament was true, inspired, and authoritative.

Prophetic

Jesus held that Scripture's prophetic truth must come to pass because it is the truth of God. In the synagogue of His home town of Nazareth our Lord read from the prophet Isaiah, then He sat down and said, "Today this scripture has been fulfilled in your hearing" (Luke 4:21). Frequently Jesus said an event would happen "for it is written" (Mark 14:27; see also Mark 9:12-13; 14:21). Then He would quote an Old Testament prophet.

Jesus told the twelve apostles, "Behold, we are going up to Jerusalem, and everything that is written of the Son of Man by the prophets will be accomplished" (Luke 18:31). As the Jews arrested Jesus, He said concerning the events leading up to that point, "All this has taken place, that the scripture of the prophets might be fulfilled" (Matthew 26:56). The Scriptures had the divine compulsion of truth that must come to pass. Earlier He said, "For I tell you that this scripture must be fulfilled in me" (Luke 22:37).

As Jesus walked with Cleopas and his companion on the road to Emmaus they were discouraged because of the death of Jesus. "We had hoped that he was the one to redeem Israel" (Luke 24:21). Jesus gently rebuked them for being slow "to believe all that the prophets have spoken! Was it not necessary that the Christ should suffer these things and enter into his glory?" (Luke 24:25-26). Later that evening on the day of his resurrection He said to the apostles, "Everything written about me in the law of Moses and the prophets and psalms must be fulfilled" (Luke 24:44). The Jews arranged the Old Testament into the Law, the Prophets and the Writings (of which Psalms was first and most prominent). Jesus was saying the whole Old Testament was prophetic of Him.

R.T. France summarized Jesus' attitude toward the Old Testament, "Jesus believed its statements, endorsed its teachings, obeyed its commands, and set himself to fulfill the pattern of redemption which it laid down."[1] Acceptance of the deity of Jesus will lead one to accept the Old Testament as true, inspired, authoritative, and prophetic.

JESUS TAUGHT THE OLD TESTAMENT WAS

1) Historically True

2) Inspired by God

3) Divinely Authoritative

4) Prophetic

Jesus' Teaching About the New Testament

It is easy to see how one's belief in the inspiration of the Old Testament can be based on Jesus' teaching. But how can confidence in the inspiration of the New Testament be based on the teaching of Jesus since no New Testament book was written until fifteen or twenty years after Jesus' return to heaven? Though Jesus could not hold up a New Testament and say, "This is the Word of God," He did promise Holy Spirit inspiration to His apostles. The apostles claimed such inspiration. The early church recognized the inspiration and authority of the apostles' word.

Promised by Jesus

Jesus promised the Holy Spirit would supernaturally guide the apostles. When Jesus was ministering in Galilee, He sent the apostles through the villages two-by-two. He said, "When they deliver you up, do not be anxious how you are to speak or what you are to speak or what you are to say; for what you are to say will be given you in that hour; for it is not you who speak, but the Spirit of your Father speaking through you" (Matthew 10:19-20).

A young preacher stopped practicing his sermons on Saturday nights at the home where he stayed. The man of the house asked why. The young man said, "I don't have to study any more. The Holy Spirit tells me what to say."

The man said, "I don't want to be disrespectful, but I wonder about that because you were preaching better sermons before." We must study Jesus' promises in context. The promises of Holy Spirit inspiration were given to the apostles, not to Christians in general.

In the sad hours of farewell at the last supper on the evening before His death, Jesus gave serious instruction and specific promises to the apostles. He promised the Holy Spirit would guide them in declaring His truth. These promises apply only to the apostles as the context indicates. Jesus told them, "He [Holy Spirit] will teach you all things, and bring to your remembrance all that I have said to you" (John 14:26; see also John 14:16-17). The "Spirit of Truth" would reveal to them the complete truth about Christ by teaching and enabling them to remember Christ's words. Jesus certified the divine origin and authority of the apostles' teaching as well as its accuracy and completeness.

Christ also assured the apostles, "He [Holy Spirit] will guide you into all truth . . . He will declare to you the things that are to come" (John 16:13; see John 16:12-15). Jesus endorsed their word. Their message would be true as His message was true, but their message would complete the revelation of the gospel. A lady once said that she did not have to obey Acts 2:38 because that was one of the apostles and not Christ talking. The Holy Spirit gave the apostles divine authority. If we accept the authority of Christ, we will accept the authority of the apostles.

Jesus promised the Holy Spirit would inspire the apostles by teaching them all things that relate to Christianity. He would supernaturally remind them of Christ's words (John 14:26). One can know what Jesus did and said through their faithful teaching and writing. The Holy Spirit would testify about Christ (John 15:26). The Holy Spirit would guide them into all truth. He would keep them from error so their message would be the truth that God wanted us to have. The apostles also were able to predict future events as God had guided the prophets of old (John 16:13).

JESUS PROMISED HOLY
SPIRIT INSPIRATION TO APOSTLES

"What you are to say will be given you in that hour; for it is not you who speak, but the Spirit of your Father speaking through you" (Matthew 10:19-20).

The Holy Spirit "will teach you all things and bring to your remembrance all that I have said to you" (John 14:26).

The Holy Spirit "will guide you into all truth . . . He will declare to you the things that are to come" (John 16:13).

Claimed by the Apostles

The preaching and writing of the apostles in the New Testament indicates that they claimed Holy Spirit guidance. When Peter preached on the Day of Pentecost, he claimed the apostles had received the promised Spirit (Acts 2:33).

Paul insisted that his gospel was not "man's gospel." "For I did not receive it from man, nor was I taught it, but it came through a revelation of Jesus Christ" (Galatians 1:12). God's message was "made known to me by revelation" (Ephesians 3:3). "It has now been revealed to his holy apostles and prophets by the Spirit" (Ephesians 3:5). In one of his earliest letters Paul said, "When you received the word of God which you heard from us, you accepted it not as the word of men but as what it really is, the word of God" (1 Thessalonians 2:13). Paul claimed that his preaching and his writing were God's word.

To the Corinthians Paul declared, "What I am writing to you is a command of the Lord (1 Corinthians 14:37). You may object that in 1 Corinthians 7:12, Paul said, "I say, not the Lord." Does he mean, "This is my human opinion which you can accept or reject"? The context rather favors the view that Paul meant, "The Lord Jesus did not say this when He was here on the earth, but as an apostle I say it to you." Paul called his teaching "the word of God" and "commandment from God"—the two expressions Jesus used about Moses' writings (Mark 7:9-13).

PAUL CLAIMED THAT HIS MESSAGE

1) Came through a revelation of Jesus Christ — Galatians 1:12
2) Was made known to him by revelation — Ephesians 3:3
3) Was revealed to the holy apostles and prophets by the Spirit — Ephesians 3:5
4) Was not the word of man but was "the word of God" — 1 Thessalonians 2:13
5) Was a command of the Lord — 1 Corinthians 14:37

We can accept the Old Testament and the New Testament books written by the apostles on the basis of Jesus' authority. How can we accept the inspiration of the books written by Luke, Mark, James, and Jude, who were not apostles? What reason can be given for accepting these books as the Word of God?

The apostles could lay hands on individuals who received miraculous gifts from the Holy Spirit. One such gift was prophecy (1 Corinthians 12:10). There were prophets in the early church in addition to the apostles (Acts 13:1; Ephesians 2:20; 3:5). The authority of the apostle Paul stands behind Luke's writing and that of Peter behind Mark's Gospel. James and the apostles claim approval from the Holy Spirit in their letter to the churches (Acts 15:13, 28). Jesus kept His promise in guiding the apostles into all truth. Part of that truth was written by non-apostles, yet they were also guided by the "Spirit of truth."

Recognized by the Early Church

Some say churchmen wrote and chose the New Testament books so the church has authority over the New Testament. But the early church merely *recognized* the books of Scripture; they did not *make* them Scripture.

Imagine with me that I have an Aunt Susie from England. I am to meet her at our local airport. She was described as short, with beautiful white hair, wears a purple coat, carries a large handbag, and has a British accent. When I see a lady who meets this description and recognize her as my Aunt Susie, I did not cause her to be Aunt Susie. I merely recognized her. The church did not make the books to be Scripture. They merely recognized and accepted the books that were inspired by the Holy Spirit.

J. I. Packer said, "The Church no more gave us the New Testament canon than Sir Isaac Newton gave us the force of gravity. God gave us gravity, by his work of creation, and similarly He gave us the New Testament canon by inspiring the individual books that make it up. Newton did not create gravity, but recognized it."[2] The New Testament books did not have to wait for later councils to be declared Scripture. Peter said of Paul's letters, "speaking of this as he does in all his letters, there are some things in them hard to understand, which the ignorant and unstable twist to their own destruction, as they do the other scriptures" (2 Peter 3:16). Peter put Paul's letters on a par with the Old Testament Scriptures. Paul quoted Luke 10:7 as Scripture in 1 Timothy 5:18.

Clement of Rome wrote the first Christian book we have outside the books of the New Testament. In his letter to the Corinthians written about A.D. 96 Clement said, "Take up the epistle of the blessed Apostle Paul. . . . Truly, under the inspiration of the Spirit, he wrote to you concerning himself, and Cephas and Apollos."[3] He said, "The apostles preached the Gospel, being full of the Holy Spirit." He called the Scripture "the true utterances of the Holy Spirit. Observe that nothing of an unjust or counterfeit character is written in them."[4] Clement affirmed the inspiration of 1 Corinthians within forty years after it was written.

Justin Martyr, writing about A.D. 140 said, "The gospels were written by men full of the Holy Spirit."[5] Irenaeus was a disciple of Polycarp, a disciple of the apostle John. Irenaeus said the gospel had come through the apostles, "which they did at one time proclaim in public, and, at a later period, by the will of God, handed down to us in the Scriptures, to be the ground and pillar of our faith."[6] He said, "the Scriptures are indeed perfect, since they were spoken by the Word of God and His Spirit."[7]

EARLY RECOGNITION OF THE INSPIRATION OF THE NEW TESTAMENT

AD 60s — Peter put Paul's letters on a par with other OT Scriptures (2 Peter 3:16)

AD 60s — Paul quoted Luke 10:7 as Scripture (1 Timothy 5:18)

AD 96 — Clement of Rome said Paul wrote 1 Corinthians under the inspiration of the Holy Spirit

AD 140— Justin Martyr said the Gospels were written by men full of the Holy Spirit

AD 180— Irenaeus said the apostles by the will of God handed down the Scriptures which were perfect since they were spoken by the Word of God and His Spirit

---

Kenneth Kantzer underscored the key issue, "The basic question about the inspiration and authority of Scripture is, 'What do you think of Christ?' If we accept him as Lord, it is consistent to submit to His teaching on the complete authority of Scripture."[8]

After Jesus fed the 5000 from the lad's lunch, the next day He taught them about the bread of life. He emphasized that following Him meant obeying His word. Many defected and followed Him no more. Jesus asked the twelve, "You do not want to go away also, do you?" (John 6:67, literal translation). Peter answered, "Lord, to whom would we go? You have the words of eternal life" (John 6:68). One can study history, philosophy, literature, psychology, science, and world religions to try to understand life. But human wisdom does not have the answers to our basic questions. Only Jesus and the Word of God can lead us to the truth of God.

In the conclusion of the Sermon on the Mount, our Lord contrasted two kinds of builders — wise and foolish. "And everyone who hears these words of mine and does not do them will be like a foolish man. . ." (Matthew 7:26). We can know the Bible, even praise it, but if we do not obey its words, we are fools. This is the fatal failure. On the other hand, "Everyone then who hears these words of mine and does them will be like a wise man . . ." (Matthew 7:24). Those who build their lives trusting and obeying the Word of God build on solid rock.

A British newspaper thought the Royal Navy was too severe in its discipline of a young man for disobedience. An old navy man wrote a letter to the editor stating that discipline is essential to learn to obey orders without question which may save one's life. He told of being on a launch towing a larger vessel in rough water. The vessel was attached to the launch by a wire hawser. Suddenly the officer-in-charge shouted, "Down!" The crew immediately fell to the deck. The wire-towing-hawser had snapped and whirled over their heads like a mad steel serpent. If the men had not instantly obeyed, they would have been instantly killed. "Obedience saved our lives."[9] This is true in the physical realm, but it is even more true in our spiritual lives.

When Jesus was on the Mount of Transfiguration, Peter suggested building three tabernacles or shelters. A cloud overshadowed them and God's voice thundered, "This is my beloved Son, with whom I am well-pleased, listen to him" (Matthew 17:5). Trust and obedience in Jesus Christ and the Word of God is the only way — the only wise, sure foundation for life. *The Bible stands true as the Word of God.*

"In the beginning God created the heavens and the earth."
Genesis 1:1

"The LORD by wisdom founded the earth; by understanding he established the heavens." *Proverbs 3:19*

"For what can be known about God is plain to them, because God has shown it to them. Ever since the creation of the world his invisible nature, namely, his eternal power and deity, has been clearly perceived in the things that have been made. So they are without excuse." *Romans 1:19-20*

"The heavens are telling the glory of God; and the firmament proclaims his handiwork." *Psalm 19:1*

"But ask the beasts, and they will teach you; the birds of the air, and they will tell you; or the plants of the earth, and they will teach you; and the fish of the sea will declare to you. Who among all these does not know that the hand of the Lord has done this." *Job 12:7-9*

"When we study the universe . . . we are led to the recognition of a Creative power . . . . to one astronomer the heavens are telling the glory of God." *W. M. Smart*

Chapter Seven
GOD STANDS TRUE IN THE UNIVERSE

PART 1 — DESIGN IN THE
PHYSICAL UNIVERSE AND IN THE HUMAN BODY

A young girl was sobbing after she had gone to bed in her suburban home in Chicago. Her father checked to see what was troubling her. That evening she had heard the TV reporter announce that some religious thinkers were saying, "God is dead." Her world was crushed. Her father assured her that though some believed that, God was very much alive.

A small boy prayed one night, "And dear God, please take care of yourself. Because if you don't, we're in a terrible fix!"

These children saw clearly what a bleak, terrible world this would be if there were no God. It would be a world without ultimate meaning and purpose in life, without absolute standards of right and wrong, and without a hope that reaches beyond the grave.

The most important knowledge a human being can have is knowledge of God. The first six chapters of this book traced the primary sources of our knowledge of God — the historical revelation of God through prophets and apostles and supremely in His Son, Jesus Christ.

The last four chapters will present two confirming lines of evidence. This chapter and the next will show evidence in nature of a Divine Designer. The last two chapters will demonstrate that Christianity stands true in the experience of life.

God stands true in the universe. The reality of God is supported by the design in the physical universe and in the human body. The wonders of God's creative handiwork are abundant in the world around us.

Gerhman Titov, a Russian Cosmonaut, asked John Glenn, one of America's astronauts, "When I was in outer space I didn't see God. Did you?"

Glenn responded, "My God isn't so small that I expected to see Him in outer space." He believed in the God who made outer space.

At Christmas time, 1968, three Americans circled the moon. *The National Geographic* observed:

> And so these three astronauts, who more than any other men have seen the evidence of creation, pause in their journey to read, in turn, the most appropriate words imaginable for the scene below them — the majestic opening words of the Book of Genesis: 'In the beginning God created the heavens and the earth . . . .' [1]

Astronaut Gordon Cooper, Jr. said, "In my opinion there is no rift between science and religion; the more one learns about scientific endeavors, the more one is convinced of the wonders of God's creation."[2] Moon-walker James B. Irwin affirmed, "I have encountered nothing on Apollo 15 or in the age of space and science that dilutes my faith in God."[3] As we learn more about the universe we have more, not less, reasons to believe in God.

Paul wrote to the Romans, "For what can be known about God is plain to them, because God has shown it to them. Ever since the creation of the world his invisible nature, namely, his eternal power and deity, has been clearly perceived in the things that have been made. So they are without excuse" (Romans 1:19-20). Even the person without the Bible should know from nature there is a supreme power and eternal deity.

When Paul was preaching in the pagan city of Lystra, he said, "He [God] did not leave himself without witness, for he did good and gave you from heaven rains and fruitful seasons, satisfying your hearts with food and gladness" (Acts 14:17). Paul appealed to the regularity in nature as a witness to God.

The Psalmist exclaimed, "The heavens are telling the glory of God; and the firmament proclaims his handiwork" (Psalm

19:1). The handiwork of God is manifested in the physical universe and in the human body.

Physical Universe

We cannot absolutely prove God from the evidence of design, but design does demand a designer. The evidence of design in the physical universe strongly points to a Creator who designed and made it all.

A British astronomer, W. M. Smart said, "When we study the universe . . . we are led to the recognition of a creative power. . . . to one astronomer the heavens are telling the glory of God."[4]

Vastness of the Universe

Astronomers tell us this universe is an extremely vast place. Light travels 186,282 miles per second. It takes light one and one fourth seconds to get from the moon to the earth. It takes eight minutes for light to come from the sun to the earth. Light traveling across our solar system takes eleven hours. Our galaxy consisting of billions of stars is 100,000 light years across.

To illustrate this vastness let each foot represent a million miles. A basketball on home plate represents the sun. The earth would be an air rifle BB 93 feet from home plate. In deep center field 484 feet away from home is a ping pong ball. That is Jupiter. If one traveled from New York City, where the basketball was on home plate, to the west coast and out into the Pacific Ocean 4,880 miles away, one would come to another basketball representing Alpha Centauri, one of the nearest stars to our sun. Each foot represents a *million* miles!

A galaxy is a huge cluster of stars. Our solar system is but a tiny speck in the giant cluster of stars, the Milky Way Galaxy — a disk-shaped spiral galaxy. Some astronomers estimate that it contains 100 billion stars.

Our galaxy, one among billions, occupies only one trillionth of known space. The universe is so vast that if this galaxy were taken out of existence there would be no greater loss to the total mass than if a pine needle were taken out of a large forest. Truly this is a vast universe.

Astronomer Robert Jastrow said that three lines of evidence have led him to conclude that the universe has an abrupt beginning — the motion of the galaxies, the laws of thermodynamics, and the life story of the stars.[5]

The authors of a college physical science textbook stated:

When we contemplate the enormous extent of space and the tremendous amount of material present, we are greatly awed. Even though we have theories regarding the development of galaxies and individual stars from gas and dust, how are we to account for all the starting material, whatever its original form? It is easy to understand why most scientists, particularly astronomers, believe in a creator.[6]

Design in the Universe

Not only is this an immense universe but it is an orderly, well-designed universe as well. The earth rotates on its axis at a tilt of 23 degrees which allows for a greater surface of the earth to be tilled and makes possible the seasons. The earth rotates at 1000 miles per hour. If it rotated at only 100 miles per hour the days and nights would be ten times longer. The summer sun would burn all vegetation and the winter's night would be incredibly cold. The earth is the right distance from the right-sized sun for life as experienced on earth. If the earth were farther away from the sun, the climate would be too cold. If the earth were closer, it would be too hot. If the sun were smaller or larger we would either freeze or roast.

Before we take the earth's moderate temperature range for granted, we should realize that on the moon in one lunar day (15 earth days) the temperature varies from a high of 214 degrees above zero to 243 degrees below zero.[7]

DESIGN IN THE UNIVERSE

Rotation of the earth on its axis
Distance of the earth from the sun and moon
Precision in the movement of the planets
Amount of oxygen in the atmosphere
Unique properties of water

The earth is the right distance from the right-sized moon for life as we know it. The ratio of the size of the moon to the earth is ten times greater than for any other planet's satellite in the solar system. If the moon were 100 times smaller, an average satellite size, its brightness would be reduced by 20 times and its influence on the earth would be greatly changed.[8]

The moon is, on an average, 240,000 miles distant from earth. The gravitational pull from the moon causes the ocean tides that cleanse our shore lines and clean out the shipping channels. If the moon were only 50,000 miles distant from the earth the gravitational pull would be so great the ocean tides would completely submerge the surface of the earth twice a day. Two baths a day, whether you need it or not! If the moon were smaller or larger it would greatly decrease or increase the ocean tides.

The precision in the movement of the planets in our solar system is so precise, scientists can calculate exactly where a planet will be hundreds of years in advance. The Naval Observatory, United States' time keeper, makes continual observation of the stars and adjusts its master clock accordingly. The best clocks and watches are adjusted to match the precision in nature. If the watch had to have a watchmaker, it is reasonable to believe that the universe also had a Maker.

The layer of gases surrounding the earth, the earth's atmosphere, also manifests design. It contains 21% oxygen. If it had 50% oxygen or more any flash of lightning would ignite a forest into fire. If we had less than 10% oxygen, fire would be unavailable to us. If the earth had no oxygen, human beings would not be able to talk about it because no organic life could exist. If the oceans were deeper and covered more ground surface, they would absorb more carbon dioxide from the air so that plant life would be jeopardized.

Water expands when it freezes. Most all other substances contract when cold and are heavier. Water expands by nine percent when it freezes. Since ice is lighter than water it floats and forms a protective barrier on top of a river or pond. If ice were heavier and formed on the bottom of a river or pond, a cold winter would cause all the water to freeze and the fish would be frozen dead. But as it is, the frozen crust over the lake protects the marine life below from the extremely cold free air above. The fish live comfortably in the constant 39 degree temperature in the water under the ice. The ocean waters absorb the heat of summer and moderate the cold of winter and vice versa.

Water is essential to life. Water dissolves more substances than any known liquid. Water enables living organisms to perform their function as chemical factories. Over 67 percent of the human body is made up of water.

The earth is unique among the planets having a significant amount of water and all 92 elements on the surface. A book advocating evolution made this admission: "In a surprising variety of ways, the properties of water — liquid water — seem almost to have been designed expressly to make the world hospitable to life."[9] Plain water points to a Designer.

Human Body

Not only is evidence of a Designer seen in the physical universe but also in the amazing structures in the human body. A professor of anatomy in a medical college said, "Every lecture in medical college is a creationist lecture whether the professor realizes it or not."

"Know that the Lord is God! It is he that made us, and we

The amazing properties of water point to a Designer.

Ants milk aphids which provide food
for the ants and keeps the aphids healthy.

are his; we are his people, and the sheep of his pasture" (Psalm 100:3).

```
DESIGN IN THE HUMAN BODY

Eye    —  Amazing camera
Ear    —  Sensitive receiver
Heart  —  Masterful pump
Brain  —  Intricate control center
Bones  —  Structural marvel
Hand   —  Flexible tool
```

The Eye

The eye is a marvel in the human body. The retina, about one square inch of tissue inside the eye, has over 100 million light-receptor cells. These fat cones and slender rods convert light into electro-chemical energy enabling a person to see.

The eye is a delicate camera that takes 16 color photos per second. It has its own light meter, protection and cleaning equipment, and self-repairing abilities. In a day's time it can take one half million pictures and instantly develop them in living color. What man-made camera can match the amazing properties of the human eye?

The Ear

Whittaker Chambers, an American Communist, documented his repudiation of communism in his autobiography, *The Witness*. He saw the essential struggle as a choice between believing in man or believing in God. He told about an experience in his Baltimore apartment that he pinpointed as the time he started doubting his atheism.[10]

He was watching his young daughter as she was eating in

her chair. He felt that she was the most miraculous thing that had happened in their lives. His eye was drawn to the delicate and intricate shape of her ears. The thought came to his mind that those ears were not the product of chance collision of atoms, which was the communist view. He concluded that they must have been the product of design. This unwanted thought forced itself into his thinking. He tried to push it out of his mind but it would not go away. As an atheist he could not acknowledge design because design presupposed God. Chambers was never able to escape the logic of the argument that design demands a Designer. Later he became a strong believer in God.

The outer ear collects the sound waves from the air and funnels them to the eardrum. The waves cause the eardrum to vibrate. The eardrum can sense frequencies that move the eardrum only one billionth of a centimeter. Vibrations are mechanically transmitted and amplified through the three connected bones in the middle ear.

The mechanical vibrations enter a fluid in the inner ear. The waves are converted into nerve impulses by the 24,000 auditory receptor cells in each ear. The auditory nerves transmit these impulses to the brain enabling a person to hear. In the space the size of a hazel nut there is enough nervous circuitry to provide phone communication for a good-sized city.

Not only does the ear enable a person to hear but it is also the organ of balance. The sensitive hair-like nerve endings in certain regions of the inner ear make possible the sense of balance.

The Heart

The heart is a twelve ounce blood pump — actually two pumps. In a day's time it beats 100,000 times, pumping 5.8 tons of blood, enough to fill a 4,000 gallon tank car. The entire circulatory system includes passageways totaling about 60,000 miles. The heart is self-lubricating, high-capacity, and self-regulating. Doctors have said that if the heart were not abused it could beat for 120 years without structural failure —

over 4 billion beats. The heart is an evidence of a Designer.

The composition of our blood cells is so complicated that in one molecule the exchange of two out of 574 amino acids can result in a dread, even fatal disease. On the basis of evolution by chance mutation, how could creatures survive while the right chemical composition of the blood was being accidentally formed?

The Brain

The human body is constructed of trillions of molecules and cells. The brain is the most complex and intricate organ in the body. It is a mass of pink-grey, jelly-like cells, weighing about three pounds. The 100 billion nerve cells in the brain subdivide into several thousand terminals making trillions of connections. Every cubic inch of the brain contains at least 100 million nerve cells interconnected by 10,000 miles of fibers. More complex than any computer, the brain can store and manipulate infinite amounts of information. It provides for conscious thought and automatic controls on the body's functioning and serves as the body's communications headquarters.

A person can see, hear, taste, smell, and touch because the brain receives the sensory impulses. Like a video tape it synchronizes sights and sounds in the brain and records thoughts and sense experience on the thread of time available to the memory for recall. The brain coordinates the physical activities in talking, walking, running, and lifting. It plays a vital role in respiration, circulation, digestion, and reproduction. It is the master control center for the body's vast, complex communication network — the nervous system.

The Bones

Our internal skeletal frame consists of 206 bones making up one-fifth of our body weight. Hard, rigid bones make possible our movements and serve the complex needs of the body. Bones are more functional than if they were solid steel or wood. They are designed to provide the greatest strength for their size and weight. Part of each major bone is dense and part is spongy. The long bones in legs and arms have a length-wise hollow in the shaft that gives strength without extra weight. The thighbone is the largest and strongest bone. A man's thighbone is strong enough to support the weight of a small car. The skeleton carries the body weight, provides protective housing for organs, and is attached to the various types of muscles for the multitude of bodily movements. Bone marrow produces one trillion red blood cells daily. The bone system has self-enclosed joints and can lubricate and repair itself.

Twenty-six bones make up the foot. Dr. Paul Brand stated, "Even when a soccer player subjects these small bones to a cumulative force of one thousand tons per foot over the course of a match, his living bones endure the stress maintaining their elasticity." And, "Our body weight is evenly spread out through architecturally perfect arches which serve as springs, and the bending of knees and ankles absorbs stress."[11]

The Hand

The human hand is an intricate, efficient piece of machinery. Because of the joints at the shoulder, elbow, wrist, and two separate bones in the forearm, the hand can make many kinds of movements. The opposable thumb makes the hand into a skilled instrument. The hand can grasp objects tightly and it can perform delicate precise movements.

Tough, flexible ligaments hold together the 27 bones in one's fingers, hand, and wrist. Their movements are produced by 30 pairs of muscles as directed by two of the larger centers of the brain. The complex arrangement of bones, ligaments, muscles, blood vessels, and nerves in the human hand is an engineering marvel that could not be a product of chance.

An adult's body has about one octillion atoms (1,000,000,000,000,000,000,000,000,000). How many is that? If our planet were a smooth ball and covered four feet deep with peas and if 250,000 other planets the size of the earth were covered four feet deep with peas, that would be one octillion peas.

What staggers the imagination is that these billions and trillions of atoms are organized into specialized cells, the cells into specialized tissues, the tissues into special organs, and organs into systems — all working together in the functioning human body. How could that happen by chance?

DNA Demands a Designer

What moves cells to work together? What ushers in the higher specialized functions of movement, sight, and consciousness through the coordination of a hundred trillion cells? The secret to membership lies locked away inside each cell nucleus, chemically coiled in a strand of DNA. Once the egg and sperm share their inheritance, the DNA chemical ladder splits down the center of every gene much as the teeth of a zipper pull apart. DNA re-forms itself each time the cell divides: 2,4,8,16,32 cells, each carries the instruction book of one hundred thousand genes. DNA is estimated to contain instructions that, if written out, would fill a thousand six-hundred-page books. A nerve cell may operate according to instructions from volume four and a kidney cell from volume twenty-five, but both carry the whole compendium. The DNA is so narrow and compacted that all genes in all my body's cells would fit into an ice cube; yet if the DNA were unwound and joined together end to end the strand could stretch from the earth to the sun and back more than four hundred times. It provides each cell's sealed credential of membership in the body. Every cell possesses a genetic code so complete that the entire body could be reassembled from information in any one of the body's cells, which forms the basis for speculation about cloning.[12]

The more scientists study living things the more they are impressed with its intricate design and beauty. The claim that all life has evolved naturally is a very unlikely theory when science has yet to explain how even one protein molecule could have come into existence by natural processes. Even if nature could produce proteins and enzymes, that would not be creating life. All life comes from life.

Scientists have developed sophisticated techniques to study living cells in minute detail. A massive amount of information is contained in the DNA molecule in a single cell and in hemoglobin, a protein in our blood that transmits oxygen through red blood cells. The DNA is a large molecule which carries hereditary information. DNA comes from DNA. Scientist Robert Gange concluded, "The calculations show that belief that life arose accidentally is statistically impossible and intellectually outrageous."[13] These scientific calculations point to God as the source of our life. Gange stated, "It is nonsensical to believe that an accident created life."[14]

Gange declared that the information contained in the material structures of the world cannot be explained without an Intelligence even if we accept the age of the earth proposed by evolutionists.

> Since the universe is simply too young and too small, to account for its appearance, (even at 13 billion years and 30 billion light-years across) we are forced to ask, "From where did it come?" The logical answer is that it came from a Supreme Intelligence! Not only is this logical, but it's also the simplest answer. If this implies religion, then this is something the individual will have to grapple with. But the irrefutable fact is that information theory and the data from electron microscopy, when applied to living cells, force the conclusion that they have been designed. Why do they force this conclusion? Because they are jam-packed with information that cannot be logically explained as the issue of natural processes within this universe.[15]

Scientific evidence points to a Designer.

A believer and an unbeliever were traveling in the Arabian

117

desert. As they discussed God, the unbeliever said he could not believe in God because he could not see God or touch Him. Their discussion ended in disagreement.

The next morning the atheist told the believer there had been a tiger in their camp. The believer responded, "I don't think so. I can't see him or touch him."

The atheist insisted, "But here are his footprints."

The believer pointed to the sunrise and said, "There is a footprint of God."

This chapter has shown many footprints of God. These evidences of design point to a Designer.

God Stands True in the Universe!

Chapter Eight
GOD STANDS TRUE IN THE UNIVERSE

PART 2 – DESIGN IN THE PLANT AND ANIMAL WORLD

We have surveyed evidence of a Designer in the physical universe and in the human body. Now we turn to the handi-work of a Designer in the plant and animal world.

In an effort to show his "miserable comforters" that they did not know it all, Job said to them, "But ask the beasts, and they will teach you; the birds of the air, and they will tell you; or the plants of the earth, and they will teach you; and the fish of the sea will declare to you. Who among all these does not know that the hand of the Lord has done this?" (Job 12:7-9).

DESIGN IN THE PLANT AND ANIMAL WORLD

Plant	—	Venus Fly Trap
Fish	—	Archer Fish
	—	Angler Fish
Birds	—	Skeleton
	—	Woodpeckers
	—	European Dippers
	—	Eagles
	—	Ducks and Geese
Engineers	—	Beavers
Migratory Animals	—	Arctic Terns
	—	Monarch Butterflies
Protective Devices	—	Ability to Act Fierce
	—	Protective Coloration
Interdependence	—	Cleaner Fish and Larger Fish
	—	Yucca Plant and Yucca Moth
Social Insects	—	Ants
	—	Bees

How can beasts, birds, plants, and fish bear witness to a Creator? One witness is through their being obviously designed for their jobs. The design in the plant and animal world points to a Designer.

Venus Fly Trap

The venus fly trap, a plant, is an intricate trap with long bristles around its edges. It gives off a sweet smelling odor that entices its prey. When an insect is tempted into the center of the plant and touches the trigger hairs, the trap snaps shut within one half second capturing the insect. The venus fly trap is an effective and delicately designed trap.

Fish

The archer fish has complex eyes that bulge out farther than those of a normal fish so it can focus both eyes on a single object. It pushes its bony tongue against the groove in the top of its mouth. Water is brought in through a quick snap of the gills and shot through this barrel and spouted at insects above the water. Allowing for water refraction and wind velocity the archer fish hits with accuracy an insect two or three feet above the water.

An evolutionist scientist writing in the *Scientific American* expressed perplexity about the archer fish. He said this ability to spout was not necessary to its survival so it was difficult to account for its development by natural selection.[1] A better explanation is that God designed it so.

The angler fish fishes for fish. It has a built-in fishing rod with a piece of flesh on the end that it uses to attract another fish. It then retracts the "bait" and promptly swallows the smaller fish. An angler fish is a poor swimmer, but with its bony, hinged pectoral fins it does well in maneuvering on the bottom of the sea. It is lumpy, squat, ugly, yet with its fishing-pole apparatus it is equipped to do what it does — fish for fish.

Birds

A bird's skeleton shows evidence of design. For flight it needs to be light but strong. The long bones are hollow and light. Internal braces give strength without adding unnecessary weight. A frigate bird with a wing span of seven feet weighs three pounds. Its entire skeleton weighs only four ounces. Air sacs add to the bird's ability to fly. They are also a part of a cooling system that allows fresh air to flow continously through the bird's body. Naturalistic scientists rave about how nature has adapted the bird for flight. But the evidence is better understood as a witness of God's designing hand.

A bird's beak is his knife, spoon, fork, hammer, and pliers all rolled up into one. Each species of birds has a beak fitted for its own way of life. The beak of the cardinal enables it to eat small seeds and grain. The flattened beak of the spoonbill works well in the mud. The needle-shaped beak of a hummingbird is effective in sipping nectar from flowers. Hawks have sharp, hooked beaks to tear flesh. Kingfishers have spears to jab their prey.

The woodpecker has a strong, chisel-shaped beak so it can bore a hole in a tree. It has an extra thick skull — a definite advantage for one who bangs its head against a tree all day. It has extra heavy shock-absorber muscles in its neck. The shock absorber tissue between the beak and skull is not found in other birds. Its two forward and two backward claws on each foot grab securely into the bark of a tree. After setting its claws, it jams its strong, spiny tail feathers into the bark to brace itself as it leans backward. When a woodpecker drums a tree it is usually looking for food. Its tongue is wrapped around the skull for additional mooring. The long, sharp tongue ends in a hard point with barbs on each side. The tongue can extend four times the length of the beak. The woodpecker can flip its tongue forward into the bark to ferret out grubs, ants, insect eggs, and hibernating insects.

The European dipper is a bird that goes through water to catch its prey. An extra-thick layer of down close to the body protects against the cold of the water. The body produces a chemical that waterproofs its feathers. Its third eyelid functions as its goggles so it can go through water with its eyes open. Tiny flaps close the nostrils while in the water. It is equipped for its job.

Birds are the only creatures with feathers. Feathers insulate the bird's body and make possible its flight. Out from the stiff shaft at the center of a feather is a web of criss-crossing and interlocking branches held together by tiny hooks. The bird is streamlined with a body that is slender and tapering. The feathers point backward from head to tail. In flight the legs, like airplane wheels, are drawn up against the body. Large, powerful chest muscles move the wings.

An eagle's wing shows the wisdom of God. We can marvel with the Proverbs writer at "the way of an eagle in the air" (Proverbs 30:18-19). The wing of an airplane causes the air to go in a whirlpool motion off the wing tip. This causes a drag and uses up energy. The primary feathers at the end of the eagle's wing can be spread apart like fingers. Instead of one large whirlpool of air this creates four to six, with less drag than one large one. The slotted wingtip enables eagles to soar and glide long distances without having to beat their wings.

The primary feathers enable birds to get forward motion. These are the only feathers that are not shaped symmetrically. The shaft is nearer to the leading edge of the feather. This uneven shape of the feather causes it to rotate back and forth as the wings go up and down. Both the upstroke and the downstroke of the wing give a forward thrust.

A scientist at the University of Oklahoma observed that "eagles' wings have some amazing aerodynamic features that have been incorporated into our large airplanes."[2] The eagle has feathered flaps that extend down at the front of its wings. They prevent stalling during flight. Usually they are folded back under the wing. Special muscles adjust them as needed; for example on one wing they may be down three or four inches and down only one inch on the other. Airplanes first had such flaps in the 1950s, but the eagle had them all along.

The airflow must continue over the wing to maintain the

uplift under the wing. When the air flow falters tufts of feathers pop up on the wing to keep the air flowing. This keeps the eagle from stalling and falling out of the sky. Airplanes have a similar mechanism.

Ducks and geese fly in a V-formation that requires less energy in flight. Just outside each bird's wing tip is a little upwash of air. The upward air wash from the bird just ahead helps each bird stay aloft, with less effort. Many birds flying in the V-formation can cut the energy needed so that the drag on each bird is only one-third of what it would be for a bird flying alone.

Beavers

The beaver has remarkable engineering skills and the physical equipment to use these skills. Its fur coat has coarse outer hairs and soft, dense underfur. Its coat sheds water and is very warm. Swimming in the winter's icy waters brings no discomfort. The beaver is a splendid swimmer and diver. On the large, partly-webbed hind feet, the second toe on each foot has a double claw to comb fur and pick splinters out from between its teeth. The front feet are small and nimble like a monkey's in order that it can pick up and carry objects.

The four large, curved incisor teeth grow throughout the beaver's lifetime and are self-sharpening. The beaver can cut through a two and one-half inch aspen branch in 30 seconds and fell a tree in almost any direction it desires. It has two protective flaps of skin behind the teeth that close off its throat cavity and keep wood chips or water out of its throat while carrying or cutting branches under water. The beaver has extra large lungs and liver so it can remain submerged for fifteen minutes. The beaver's small ears and nose have valves that close when submerged. It uses its flat, scaly tail as a brace when sitting upright, a rudder when swimming, and a device to warn the colony by hitting the water with it.

Beavers build a dam, thus providing a pond where the water level is constant. They do not make the dam completely water tight but allow enough seepage to keep the water fresh.

They build a dome-shaped lodge of tightly woven sticks. Before winter arrives the lodge is plastered with mud. When frozen, it keeps the cold wind out. The entrances open well below the water level so the beavers can go in and out below the winter's ice. The water entrance and exit protect against land enemies. The living area is above the water, thus protecting against water enemies.

The beaver did not have to go to the Massachusetts Institute of Technology to learn these amazing engineering abilities for its logging and carpentering work.

Migratory Animals

Many animals have uncanny instincts that guide them in routes of migration. The arctic tern makes yearly flights from its arctic breeding grounds to near the South Pole. It flies the 11,000 mile three-month journey without getting lost. What is it that guides it in its flight pattern? God designed this bird with the instinct to fly exactly to its destination.

Monarch butterflies are beautiful insects. In the fall millions of monarchs leave their breeding grounds in the northern United States and fly south to California, Texas, Mexico, and Florida. Each year in October a few million monarchs come to Pacific Grove, California and winter in six acres of pines. The new generation that comes each year has never been there before but they choose the same trees as their parents. The instinct that guides them to these never-before-visited wintering places is an evidence of a Designer.

Protective Devices

The ability to act fierce which helps protect some animals from predators is seen by some as an evidence of survival of the fittest. The issue between creation and evolution is not the survival of the fittest but the *arrival* of the fittest. It is more reasonable that God designed creatures with these abilities than that nature adapted them by chance.

The Io moth seems defenseless. But when it opens its wings, the fake eyes on the under wings might cause a bird to do a double-take before eating the moth. An owl can puff up several times its normal size making it look fierce. By gulping seawater the porcupine fish expands its body with spines sticking out all over. This discourages larger fish from swallowing it. A praying mantis is an insect that looks like a vicious monster. In fact, it is a very beneficial insect.

Other animals are protected because of disguise, as their colors and patterns match their surroundings. Why couldn't God have designed them this way? The striped tiger merges with a background of dark and light stalks. The dark and light coloration of a woodcock makes it camouflaged in the leaves. A grey moth is hard to detect on a mossy tree. Desert toads are almost hidden from sight in the desert sand. A bumble bee moth enjoys protection because it looks like a bumble bee.

The ptarmigan is a bird that lives in the northern United States and Canada. In the warm part of the year it wears a coat of speckled brown feathers. In the fall molt it loses these feathers. White feathers grow back that disguises the ptarmigan in its snowy habitat. It even grows white feathers between its toes to protect against frostbite.

Interdependence

Many cases of interdependence may be seen in nature. Several kinds of shrimp and small fish are cleaners. Often brightly colored, they attract the larger fish. The cleaner then goes over the body of the fish, biting off parasites, even making tiny incisions to remove those below the skin. It also cleans the gills and mouth cavity. Fish often stand in line waiting to be cleaned. It keeps the larger fish healthy and provides food for the cleaners.

The partnership between the yucca plant and the yucca moth is one of the most beautiful and amazing in nature.

They need each other. The plant cannot pollinate itself so it needs help from the moth. The moth cannot get along without the yucca bloom on which it lives. And the plant provides housing and food for the eggs and larva stage of the moth. The pollen must get into the tube-like stigma that hangs down in the flower. The pollen is sticky and cannot be blown by the wind or carried by a chance insect. The adult yucca moths appear at the right time for the plant to be pollinated. With its specially curved mouth parts the moth gathers the pollen and rolls it into a ball that is carried under her chin. She then sticks her egg-laying tube into the seed-producing part of the plant and lays her eggs. She then stuffs the ball of pollen she has been carrying into the tube of the stigma, thus insuring the reproduction of the plant. The yucca seeds develop in the pods and the larvae hatch from the eggs. The larvae eat only a few of the seeds, leaving plenty to reproduce the plant. If the plant and the moth arose by chance, there had to be mutations at the same time. The evidence fits better the view that they were designed by a Creator to work together.

Social Insects

Ants are amazing insects that show the wisdom of God. Soldier ants have protruding mandibles that can squirt a gummy substance, entangling the feet of their enemies. Some ants have a stinger at the tip of the abdomen. The queen's job is to lay eggs for the colony. When she dies, a special food is given to a female in the colony who then develops into a queen. Most ants are workers, wingless, non-egg laying females. They feed, care for, and protect the queen and her offspring. If a 150-pound man were as strong as an ant he could lift 67,000 pounds. Among insects, ants are some of the strongest and busiest.

Ants often run a "dairy." They protect and "pasture" aphids. They "milk" aphids by stroking the aphid's abdomen with their antennae. This causes the aphid to give off a honey-dew liquid that is food for the ant and keeps the aphid healthy. Sometimes they build "barns" to shelter the aphids. And of course the aphids eat on our gardens.

The bee may be the most useful insect for man. Bees are the only insects that produce food eaten by man. Beeswax is used in making several products. Bees are essential to the pollination of many fruit trees, alfalfa and clover plants, and many garden vegetables.

There are three castes of bees: the queen who lays the eggs, the males who mate with the queen and the most interesting and intelligent caste, the workers who are females who cannot lay eggs. The workers do all the work in the colony.

The worker develops from an egg laid in the cell of the honeycomb. After going through the larva and pupa stage, the adult workers emerge. They change their activity as they grow older. For the first ten days they clean house in the comb. For the next ten days they are the nurses in the colony feeding the larvae, the males and the queen using a food manufacturing gland in their heads. During the next period they become the defenders of the colony and builders as their wax-making glands develop. The worker bee spends its last stage hunting and gathering pollen and nectar.

One group of workers gathers only pollen, another group gathers only nectar. The pollen collectors fill their honey stomach before they leave the comb. They moisten the pollen they find with honey so it will stick to hairs on their body and legs. They scrape the pollen with their pollen combs and then stuff it into the pollen baskets on their back legs.

Scout bees inform other workers of the location, quantity, and quality of a supply of nectar by a certain dance they do and the sounds they make. The nectar collectors put the nectar into their honey stomachs. When they return home with the stay-at-home workers they produce honey from the nectar.

After the nurse stage, the feeding glands contract and the wax glands mature. Flakes of wax ooze from between the segments of the abdomen which are put in the mouth and chewed and then fashioned into the comb. The cells in the comb are six-sided in shape fitting snugly against each other on all sides, providing structural strength and maximum capacity.

The honeybee is designed for efficiency. On the back leg is the pollen basket. The lower part of the legs is used as pollen combs. The spur on the center leg is used in unloading pollen and in removing the wax from the glands on the abdomen. Each front leg has a special joint with a comb for cleaning the eyes and a notch for cleaning the antennae when clogged with pollen.

Running from the Designer

Charles Darwin was sent to Cambridge University in England by his father with the hope Charles would become a minister. While there he read William Paley's *Natural Theology*, which presented the evidence for God from design. While in college Darwin lost his faith in the Bible and looked for a natural explanation for the origin of living things. The rest of his life was a flight from Paley's God. Darwin admitted the discomfort that the apparent design in the human eye and a peacock's feather gave to him, yet he discounted this

---

CHARLES DARWIN ON DESIGN IN THE EYE

"To suppose that the eye, with all its inimitable contrivances for adjusting the focus to different distances, for admitting different amounts of light, and for the correction of spherical and chromatic aberration, could have been formed by natural selection, seems, I freely confess, absurd in the highest possible degree." (*The Origin of Species,* 1859)[3]

"I remember well the time when the thought of the eye made me cold all over, but I have got over this stage of the complaint, and now trifling particulars of structure often make me very uncomfortable. The sight of a feather in a peacock's tail, whenever I gaze at it, makes me sick." (*Letter to Asa Gray,* 1860)[4]

---

evidence. He developed and popularized a view of evolution of all species by natural selection resulting from the survival of the fittest. Many have been convinced that amoeba-to-man evolution is established scientific fact.

Evolutionists have said that man has evolved from an animal ancestry. The popular chart showing a progression from small ape-like animals up to man is under serious attack by scientists. No conclusive proof has been established that man has evolved from an animal ancestry. In the discredited chart of so-called ape-men, *Australopithecus* and on down are clearly apelike animals. *Homo erectus* and on up are clearly human beings. A line can be drawn with animals on one side and man on the other. Producing a chart from monkey to man furnished no proof that man evolved from ape-like ancestors or from any other animal. When humans first appear in the fossil record they are fully human. Men have always been men and apes have always been apes.

The story that Charles Darwin was converted on his death bed lacks good historical support. However, Darwin stated his thoughts in a letter written near the end of his life. He said that at the time he wrote *Origin of Species* he believed in a "First cause having an intelligent mind." This belief grew weaker. He stated, "But then arises the doubt, can the mind of man, which has, as I fully believe, been developed from a mind as low as that possessed by the lowest animals, be trusted when it draws such grand conclusions?"[5] When a person wrote to Darwin affirming that the universe is not a product of chance, Darwin responded:

> But then with me the horrid doubt always arises whether the convictions of man's mind, which has been developed from the mind of lower animals, are of any value or at all trustworthy. Would any one trust in the convictions of a monkey's mind, if there are any convictions in such a mind?[6]

Darwin used and trusted his mind in developing his theory of evolution. But when his mind suggested the idea of a Creator he suddenly could not trust his mind.

Julian Huxley, an influential evolutionary biologist, in

Evolution in Action said that the odds against evolving an animal such as a horse by pure chance alone would be the number 1 followed by 3 million zeros. It would take 3 books 500 pages each to write the figure. Huxley says about the statistical odds "Of course this could not really happen. . . . One with three million noughts after it is the measure of the unlikeliness of the horse — the odds against it happening at all. No one would bet on anything so improbable happening; and yet it has happened."[7] Those who say evolution is based on facts and creation is based only on faith need to realize that both views involve faith.

A group of biologists and mathematicians met at Wistar Institute in 1967 to study the mathematical odds for mutations in natural selection to serve as a cause for evolutionary change. Even though all participants were evolutionists they concluded the statistical odds were against mutations accounting for evolutionary change. The fact that they continued to affirm evolution and reject creation indicates that they held to evolution by faith.[8]

The Reasonableness of Belief in God

One may be embarrassed by the question, "Who made God?" But something had to be in existence eternally for other things to come from it. Either matter or a mind is eternal.

It is more reasonable to believe that a Mind is eternal and has created the world and other minds than it is to believe that matter is eternal and by natural processes developed the universe and minds. Scientific evidence opposes the idea that matter is eternal. The second law of thermodynamics states the principle that all energy and matter in the universe is moving irreversibly toward increasing disorder. Since the universe has not reached a state of total disorder, it cannot have existed forever. This law of science implies that the universe had a beginning when it was given order and energy.

Two of Britain's leading scientists, Chandra Wickramasinghe and Fred Hoyle, announced that their research had convinced them that the evidence did not support Darwinian evolution that life arose spontaneously. They calculated that the chances of life arising spontaneously would be only one in $10^{40,000}$. They said the chances of this happening are the same as for a Boeing 747 jet plane being formed by a tornado rearranging a junkyard.[9] Driven to accept an intelligence behind the universe, they concluded: "There must be a God."[10]

A small boy walked out on an old dock by a river and held up and waved a red flag. A skeptical stranger asked, "You don't think that steamboat will stop for a little fellow like you, do you?"

The boy confidently responded, "I certainly do." The boat did pull over and stop and put out a gang plank. Just before the boy walked up the board he said with a twinkle in his eye, "I knew it would stop. You see, my Daddy is the captain of that boat!" That made all the difference in the world.

The person who comes to realize the wisdom and power of God might well cower in terror and dread. But the Creator of the universe has shown Himself to be our Father, loving and compassionate. God becomes real in our lives when we accept Jesus as Lord and Savior. *God Stands True in the Universe.*

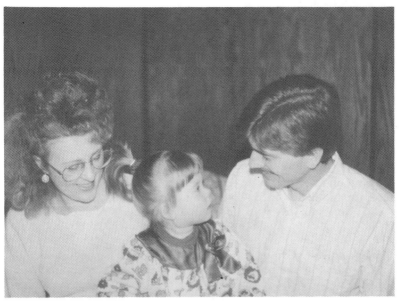

Christ teaches us to love one another
which is the basis for healthy families.

Christ gives us a hope that sustains us in life.

"If you continue in my word, you are truly my disciples, and you will know the truth, and the truth will make you free . . . . If the Son makes you free, you will be free indeed." *John 8:32*

"You shall love the Lord your God with all your heart, and with all your soul, and with all your mind and with all your strength . . . . You shall love your neighbor as yourself." *Mark 12:30-31*

"May the God of hope fill you with all joy and peace in believing, so that by the power of the Holy Spirit you may abound in hope." *Romans 15:13*

"Our hearts are restless until they rest in thee." *Augustine*

"Give up yourself, and you will find your real self. Lose your life and you will save it. Submit to death, death of your ambitions and favourite wishes every day and death of your whole body in the end: submit with every fibre of your being, and you will find eternal life. Keep back nothing. Nothing that you have not given away will ever be really yours. Nothing in you that has not died will ever be raised from the dead. Look for yourself, and you will find in the long run only hatred, loneliness, despair, rage, ruin, and decay. But look for Christ and you will find Him; and with Him everything else thrown in." *C. S. Lewis*

Chapter Nine
CHRISTIANITY STANDS TRUE IN LIFE

PART 1 — MEANING AND FREEDOM

The direct line of evidence for Christianity is the historical case for the deity of Jesus and His testimony that the Bible is the Word of God. Confirming evidence in the universe supports the reality of a Creator who designed this world. In this chapter we will see that experience in life also confirms the truth of Christianity. Christ meets the needs of the human heart. The proof of the pudding is in the eating. The final proof of Christianity is in the *living*. Jesus said that if we honestly desire to do the will of God we will know that Christ's teaching is truly of God (John 7:17).

A little boy, bent over double with stomach pain, said to his friends, "Don't eat any of those green apples."

They protested, "Why not?"

He responded, "Because they will give you a stomachache. And I have inside information to prove it!"

Christian believers have inside information in their lives that assures them Christianity stands true. The final proof is in the living. The urgent question used to be, "Is there life after death?" Now many are asking, "Is there life after birth?" None of us asked to be born. But we do want to live. We want to live a worthwhile life.

A young man on the west coast expressed this quest for life,

> We look for the basis of life in a materialistic society of money, sex, drugs, fame, and put-ons—without success. These give a temporary life, but it doesn't last. It's like trying to catch a bubble. You see it, reach for it and it bursts at your touch. We are looking for a bubble that won't burst. Where is it?[1]

There is One who can answer life's questions. Jesus said, "I came that they may have life, and have it abundantly" (John 10:10). Believers have found "a worthy and full life in Christ" (Colossians 1:10).

An older man stopped his Lincoln Continental behind a stalled Ford car and asked the stranded motorist, "What's the trouble?" The man told him the problem.

The old gentleman tinkered a bit under the hood and said, "Now, try it." The car worked fine.

"Who are you, anyway?" the grateful motorist asked.

"I'm Henry Ford," came the reply. The man who designed and made the car knew how to fix it.

Jesus is the one who knows what life is all about and can give us the best life. He is the best qualified authority on life because he created us (John 1:1-3) and because he lived a perfect life (2 Corinthians 5:21). "In him was life" (John 1:4). He "is our life" and has "all the treasures of wisdom and knowledge" (Colossians 3:4; 2:3).

Jesus answers the basic questions about life. The Christian life is not dull and uneventful. Jesus offers the most exciting and worthwhile life. It is only in Him that we can experience life to the fullest.

Meaning

We cry out for meaning and purpose in life. What is life all about? Who am I? Why am I here on this earth? Where am I going? What is my purpose for living?

A campus minister was teaching evidences for the reality of God in a university dormitory. A student, who was on the floor, rolled over, looked up, and exclaimed, "Boy, this could really grab you and make you think there really is something to life." Christ does make life worth living!

Many have not found the answer to meaning in life. They are confused and frustrated at the despair of the meaningless treadmill of their life. They try to ignore and escape their lostness through drugs, entertainment, and new experiences.

Several influential thinkers in the nineteenth century have contributed to modern man's confusion about who he is. Perhaps Karl Marx has influenced more people in the last 150 years than any other person who has lived during that time. Marx denied the existence of God. He considered himself a humanist. He believed that human beings are only physical beings shaped by economics. He believed that we are matter that eats. Man has no eternal spirit. No ethical standards are valid except whatever works for the good of the classless society.

Charles Darwin, a second influential thinker, lost his faith in God and the Bible. He concluded that man was not created in the image of God but was the product of the evolutionary processes of nature directed only by chance. People were reduced to the level of complex animals. If we are merely animals then we can breed a super race and kill off the unwanted. People who view themselves as merely animals soon begin living by barnyard ethics. It is true that the human body has some things in common with animals but human beings are unique and distinct from animals because we are made in the image of God.

Frederick Nietzsche was a brilliant (and at times insane) German thinker. In one of his books, he described a madman who rushed into the town market carrying a lantern crying, "I seek God!" The bystanders taunted him that maybe God was lost or hiding. Then the madman shouted, "Where is God?" Then he answered his own question, "We have killed Him!" He continued, "Is there any up and down left? Are we not straying as through an infinite nothing?"[2] His conclusion was that "God is dead."[3]

For Nietzsche, moral standards did not exist since God did not exist. In his book, *Beyond Good and Evil,* he ridiculed Christian morality as weak and insisted that might makes right. Man is amoral. There is no right or wrong. A twentieth century atheist, Jean-Paul Sartre, said he was forlorn that God did not exist, but because no God exists everything is permitted.[4] This view can be vividly illustrated. If one wants to help a crippled lady across the street, fine. If he wants to smash her teeth down her throat, that's okay too. Anything goes in a world without meaning.

The influential psychologist, Sigmund Freud, said, "Only religion can answer the question of purpose of life. One can hardly be wrong in concluding that the idea of having a purpose stands and falls with the religious system."[5] He viewed religion as a childish refusal to face reality. Since he denied the reality of God, he viewed guilt as only an emotional maladjustment created by the repressive tactics of traditional morality. The sinner becomes a patient. Man is shaped and determined by the inner drives of his subconscious mind. He promoted the view that the sexual instinct is the driving force behind all human action. Genuine free will and moral responsibility are lost because we are entirely conditioned and programmed by our heredity and environment.

These ideas have greatly influenced how modern people feel about themselves.

These ideas were taught in twentieth century Germany

WHAT IS A HUMAN BEING?

Karl Marx — Matter That Eats
He denied God and all spiritual realities.We are reduced to material machines shaped by economics.

Charles Darwin – Complex Animal
He denied that we were created in the image of God who became a sinner in need of a Savior. We are reduced to being accidents of nature who are merely physical and chemical organisms.

Frederick Nietzsche — Amoral Being
Since he denied God existed, he also rejected any ultimate moral standard of goodness. He emphasized will and power believing that might makes right. Do whatever you will to do.

Sigmund Freud – Shaped by His Inner Drives
Rejecting religious explanations, he explained man in terms of the psychology of his inner drives, especially the sexual instinct. We are not genuinely free or morally responsible because we are programmed by our heredity and environment.

with disastrous results. Adolf Hitler had the audacity to act on the basis of these ideas. Hitler may be, in some respects, the representative twentieth-century man for western culture. If no God exists, we are only complex physical animals programmed by our chemistry and environment. If this is true, then why not breed a master race and kill off the unwanted? The loss of belief in God in the western world has resulted in a loss of purpose and meaning, the loss of spiritual values and moral standards. War and man's inhumanity to man are the bitter fruit.

This attitude of confusion and despair has often expressed itself in modern art. A small boy with his mother at an art museum looked at a painting every way. He finally asked, "Mom, what is it?"

She read the inscription and answered, "It's supposed to be an Indian on a horse."

He looked at his mother, no-nonsense-like, "Well, if it's supposed to be, why isn't it?" We may at times be perplexed why some paintings appear so unreal and strange.

Francis Bacon, a contemporary British artist, painted a caricature of a famous painting of a pope. It expressed not so much of his view of the pope as it did his view of humanity. Bacon pictured man as irrational — the head is flying apart. He is boxed in a neurotic cage. The mouth cries out in helplessness and hopelessness. Bacon explained, "Man now realizes that he is an accident, that he is a completely futile being, that he has to play out the game without reason." Religious possibilities have been canceled for man. "Man now can only attempt to beguile himself for a time, by prolonging his life — by buying a kind of temporary immortality through the doctors." "Art has become a game by which man distracts himself."[6] Bacon expressed through his art his view of life without God.

In a godless world people are confused, aimless, hopeless, without standards. Life is without any ultimate meaning. Man is lost. Instead of rejecting modern unbelievers with disgust, we need to reach out to them in love with the good news of hope. Even those who have lost their way are not to be considered junk for some human trash heap. Lost men and women are not worthless rubbish for the garbage dump.

Each person is important and valuable because he or she is made in the image of God and because Christ died for each one. God made each person as a spiritual being for fellowship with Him. God cares for us so much that Christ came to earth to die to make available new life with God. No one should say, "I am worthless." Jesus gives us a life worth living.

Pascal observed that all men have a desire for happiness that is not satisfied by this present world. There is within each individual a "mark and empty trace" which he vainly tries to fill with things from this world. These are inadequate because this empty place can only be filled by God, Himself.[7] Augustine centuries earlier wrote, "Our hearts are restless until they rest in thee."[8]

Dorothy Sayers described the sin of our age that "believes in nothing, cares for nothing, seeks to know nothing, interferes with nothing, enjoys nothing, hates nothing, finds purpose in nothing, lives for nothing, and remains alive because there is nothing for which it will die."[9]

A Princeton University young man demonstrated against the draft by holding a sign that read, "Nothing is worth dying for." Those who do not hold any convictions for which they would die usually do not see any ultimate purpose and meaning to their lives. They try to escape in drugs, alcohol, sexual experience, and entertainment. Expensive homes often house those who have too much to live with but too little to live for.

A desire exists in the heart of every person that this world cannot satisfy. Only God can satisfy that desire. If God is real, Christ is Lord, and the Bible true, then life is worth living as we seek to glorify God by doing His will. Real happiness comes from knowing God. "Take delight in the Lord, and he will give you the desires of your heart" (Psalm 37:4).

Restless people try to "find themselves." We find meaning in life not by seeking ourselves but by seeking and finding God. In surrender of self and trust and obedience to Christ we find our true identity. When we know our Creator and

Lord, we know ourselves and can give our lives in meaningful service to God and to our fellow man.

Freedom

The desire for freedom is one of the deepest drives of the human spirit. Freedom is hard to achieve and easy to lose. In the last seven or eight centuries, western civilization has seen struggles for economic, religious, political, racial, and social freedom. Liberation movements have punctuated our times.

FREEDOM

Freedom Is Not
  Doing as You Please
  Absence of Rules

Freedom Is the
  Ability to Do What You Were Meant to Do

A four-year-old boy hopped up on his daddy's knee and asked, "Dad, how old do I have to be before I can do as I please?"

Wisely the father responded, "I don't know. Nobody ever lived that long."

We never reach a position where we can completely do as we please. Rules and responsibilities to others limit our total freedom. A supreme court justice must stop his or her car for a school traffic boy. An 80-year-old woman must put a stamp on her letter. The person who tries to do completely as he or she pleases is ruled by a severe dictator — a selfish will.

When Jamaica received its independence from England in 1962 a Jamaican said, "When we get our independence, I'm going to drive my car down the wrong side of the street in

Kingston to show we're free." A friend reminded him, "Yes, and you will be stopped by an independent policeman and pay an independent fine in an independent court." Freedom has limits and responsibilities.

Freedom is not an absence of rules. A young man fed up with his parents' rules left home and joined the Marines. He soon learned he had not escaped rules.

Would the absence of traffic laws in downtown traffic at rush hour in a large city result in freedom? No! It would mean chaos. The laws make possible the freedom to drive.

Not everyone is free to play beautiful music on a piano. Those are free to play who have disciplined themselves to obey the rules of harmony and can strike the right notes at the right time. Real freedom involves obeying basic rules.

To be free to play baseball, one must play according to the rules. When boys are playing ball in an open lot and they cannot agree on the rules, usually a quarrel results and everyone goes home mad.

In football the rules allow you to tackle and knock down an opponent. But in basketball the referees frown on it. They blow their whistle and call a foul when you knock another player down. To be free to play the sport you must play by the rules.

A robin who had two little ones decided it was time for flying lessons. She nudged the little birds out of the nest onto a ledge. When she told them to fly they sat there like bumps on a log. The mother robin dive-bombed one of the small robins and forced it to fly. It floundered and grabbed onto a limb of a dying elm tree. She knocked him off the limb and made him fly again. It was not long until he was flying fairly well. She repeated the process with the other robin.

What if before the feathers were developed on their wings those two small robins had decided they wanted to escape their confinement in the nest? If they had hopped out of the nest and tried to fly before they were ready, they would not be free to fly. They would be free to be a meal for the neighborhood cat.

Freedom is the ability to do what one is meant to do. We

are truly free when we can be the kind of persons God intended. True freedom means doing what God designed us to do.

The worldly-wise say a Christian is in a straitjacket and cannot have fun. Many non-Christians profess to be free and can do as they please. Who is really free? The person who can say no to drink and drugs or the person who cannot say no? Who is free? The person who can say no to sexual sin or the person who cannot say no to selfish lusts? Who is free? Those who can reject arrogance, hatred, and dishonesty or those who are controlled by these? Many who boast of their freedom are merely rattling their chains. Choosing to sin does not make one truly free. Jesus said, "Everyone who continues sinning is a slave to sin" (John 8:34, literal translation). Sinning does not lead to freedom but rather to slavery. Peter said of ungodly leaders, "They promise them freedom, but they themselves are slaves of corruption; for whatever overcomes a man, to that he is enslaved" (2 Peter 2:19).

Aldous Huxley admitted that he was unwilling to submit to the demands of Christian living. He said,

> I had motives for not wanting the world to have a meaning; consequently assumed that it had none, and was able without difficulty to find satisfying reasons for this assumption. The philosopher who finds no meaning in the world is . . . concerned to prove that there is no valid reason why he personally should not do as he wants to . . . . For myself, the philosophy of meaninglessness was essentially an instrument of liberation, sexual and political.[10]

But Huxley's lifestyle of so-called freedom, involving drugs, adultery, and mysticism did not bring him happiness.

Jesus told of a young man who wanted to be free from his parents so he could do as he pleased. Perhaps he said to his father one day, "I've had it. I'm sick and tired of you and Mom bossing me around — telling me when to go to bed, when to get up, where I can go, what I can wear. I want my inheritance now and I want to get out of this place. I'm going to have fun and be free."

Sadly the father gave him his share of inheritance. The young man headed for the bright lights in the big city. He wasted his money in sinful living. When his money ran out, his friends left. He ended up in a pigpen — feeding pigs. That's a bad place for a Jewish boy.

"He came to himself" (Luke 15:17). He thought, "I came out here to be free and have fun. Look at me, I'm worse off than the servants in my father's house." He decided to return home and made up a speech to give to his father. "I've sinned against God and you. I'm no longer worthy to be an important part of the family as a son. I want to come back and obey your will as a servant."

He headed home not knowing how his father would receive him. His loving father saw him afar off and ran and fell on his neck and kissed him many times. The father told the servants to kill the fatted calf and prepare a banquet. He told them to bring fine clothes — robe, ring, shoes — and music for the time of rejoicing.

As the son shared in the celebration, he might have thought, "I left because I wanted to be free but I ended up as a slave. Now I've come home in submission to my father and I've found real freedom." Jesus said, "If you continue in my word, you are truly my disciples, and you will know the truth, and the truth will make you free . . . If the Son makes you free, you will be free indeed" (John 8:31-32,36).

The truth of God does not enslave us but rather it frees us from selfishness and sin. It frees us to be the kind of persons God intended for us to be. Christ did not please Himself (Romans 15:3). Christ called us to freedom but He does not want us to use our freedom as a license to misuse one another but rather "through love to be servants of one another" (Galatians 5:13).

Freedom is the liberty to do what we know we ought to do. What is right with God is best for us. God does not limit us from what is good but He wants to protect us from what is bad for us. He liberates us to do what is good. Real freedom means we can say no to sin and yes to doing what is right with God. Submission to the will of God is the way to true freedom (Romans 6:17-18, 22).

Christ meets our need for meaning and purpose in life by giving us a life worth living. "Whatever you do, do all to the glory of God" (1 Corinthians 10:31).

Christ meets our desire for freedom. He can set us free from sin and death and free us to walk in His righteousness (Romans 8:1-4). *Christianity Stands True in Life!*

Chapter Ten
CHRISTIANITY STANDS TRUE IN LIFE

PART 2 — PEACE, LOVE, HOPE

When men do not know God, they do not know how to treat their fellow man. Aleksandr Solzhenitsyn spoke about the cause of the Russian communist revolution:

> I have spent well-nigh 50 years working on the history of the Russian Revolution; in the process I have collected hundreds of personal testimonies, read hundreds of books, and contributed eight volumes of my own. But if I were asked today to formulate as concisely as possible the main cause of the ruinous revolution that swallowed up some 60 million of our people, I could not put it more accurately than to repeat: 'Men have forgotten God.'[1]

He said if he were to identify the principal trait of the entire twentieth century it would be that "we have lost touch with our Creator."

By knowing Christ we know God. We find meaning and purpose for our lives. We experience the freedom to be the man or woman God designed us to be. Christ helps us know how to love one another and how to live in peace. He gives us hope for the future. Christ meets the deepest needs of the human heart.

Peace

We want peace — peace of mind, peace in our world. Yet so many things break the peace. War with its ugly face is always with us. Disrespect, disobedience, and divorce divide and destroy families. Civil strife, labor-management confrontations, urban riots, and selfish power-hungry persons are common.

We will never have real peace in our hearts and homes and in this world until we first find peace with God. Sin makes one an enemy of God. "There is no peace, says the Lord, for the wicked" (Isaiah 48:22). One may have a cold war in his heart with God — holding Him at arm's length — or be openly rebellious and disobedient. Real peace is denied to those who do not know God.

Jesus said, "My peace I give you" (John 14:27). To all who will come and learn of Him, He offers rest for their souls (Matthew 11:28-30). Paul said Jesus is our peace breaking down the wall of hostility, thus making peace and reconciling us with God (Ephesians 2:14-15).

"Since we are justified by faith, we have peace with God through our Lord Jesus Christ" (Romans 5:1). There must be a change within us as we come to Jesus in simple, humble trust. Coming to Him in faith, repentance, and baptism we have a clean conscience, a sense of wholeness, and a peace that cannot be expressed in words (John 8:24; Acts 2:38; Romans 6:3-6; 2 Corinthians 5:16; 1 Peter 3:21). A Christian would not take a million dollars for being able to lay his head on the pillow at night knowing all is well with God.

David described this peace in Psalm 40:

I waited patiently for the LORD;
    he inclined to me and heard my cry.
He drew me up from the desolate pit,
    out of the miry bog,
and set my feet upon a rock,
    making my steps secure.
He put a new song in my mouth,
    a song of praise to our God.
Many will see and fear,
    and put their trust in the LORD (Psalm 40:1-3).

Isaiah said, "Thou dost keep him in perfect peace, whose mind is stayed on thee, because he trusts in thee" (Isaiah

26:3). The Christian finds real contentment as he daily prays, worshiping and walking with his God. Real peace starts with peace with God.

If we have peace with God, then we can live with ourselves. God will give us inner peace and strength to deal with our problems. God erases the guilty cry of our consciences. He can take away self-hatred, loneliness, and fear.

H. G. Spafford was sailing for England to get his wife. Part of his family died in an ocean liner accident. His wife had telegrammed, "Saved. Alone." When his ship passed the area of the wreck, he went to his cabin and wrote:

> When peace, like a river, attendeth my soul,
> When sorrows like sea billows roll;
> Whatever my lot, Thou hast taught me to say,
> It is well, It is well with my soul.

Everyone has problems. No one is trouble-free. The real difference in people is in how they handle their problems. Some people let their troubles make them bitter. Others who have peace with God find themselves made better through troubles.

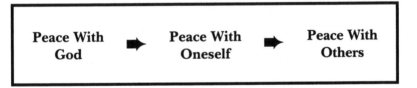

When we have peace with God and with ourselves then, in so far as it is up to us, we can live at peace with others. The person who is not at peace with himself often has conflict with others. James said, "What causes wars, and what causes fightings among you? Is it not your passions that are at war in your members? You desire and do not have; so you kill. And you covet and cannot obtain; so you fight and wage war" (James 4:1-2). The real enemy of peace is selfishness. Those who seek only to please themselves do not find peace.

Abraham Lincoln was walking down the street with a son

on each side. Both were crying loudly. A stranger asked, "Mr. Lincoln, what's the matter?" Lincoln shook his head sadly, "Same thing that is the matter with the whole world. I have three walnuts and they each want two."

It is impossible to avoid some conflict in life. But when we have peace with God, and peace with ourselves, then God will give us strength to live at peace with others. "If possible, so far as it depends upon you, live peaceably with all" (Romans 12:18). A person of peace is not merely a yes-man always agreeing with anything. Rather Christ gives strength to act in love toward others rather than lash back in revenge.

A man purchased a newspaper at a convenience store. The salesperson answered the man's "Good evening" with an unpleasant response including a curse. As they walked off, his companion asked, "How did you keep from losing your temper?" The man responded, "Why should I let him determine my behavior?"

Christ not only gives peace, but He enables His followers to be peacemakers. "Blessed are the peacemakers, for they shall be called sons of God" (Matthew 5:9). "And the peace of God, which passes all understanding, will keep your hearts and your minds in Christ Jesus" (Philippians 4:7). "Let the peace of Christ rule in your hearts" (Colossians 3:15).

Love

The songwriter wrote, "What the world needs now is love, sweet love." All would agree. We need love. A British atheistic philosopher, Bertrand Russell, in discussing the only hope for the world admitted:

> The thing I mean — please forgive me for mentioning it is love, Christian love or compassion. If you feel this, you have a motive for existence, a guide in action, a reason for courage, an impressive necessity for intellectual honesty. If you feel this, you have all that anybody should need in the way of religion. Although you may find happiness you will never know the deep despair of those whose life is aimless and void of purpose.[2]

Russell spent his life attacking belief in God, cutting down the root of faith in God. Yet, he needs love that is the fruit of faith in God. A flower cut from its root soon dies. A person cut off from God cannot maintain an unselfish love for others.

An evolutionary anthropologist said, "That love is an essential part of the nourishment of every baby and that unless he is loved he will not grow and develop as a healthy organism."[3] He noted that in the early decades of the twentieth century most infants in institutions died because of the lack of mother love. A great tragedy of our day is that many children are growing up unloved, with parents more interested in their personal pleasure and creature comforts.

Today's women are told that they must have a career to be fulfilled. However, mothers are the key influence in shaping the character and basic values of their children. Mothers, whether they are employed outside the home or not, must genuinely love their children and rise to the challenge of the ministry of motherhood.

Not only do children need mothers who love them, they also need fathers who love them. Fathers must not use their job as an excuse to put all the discipline, decision-making, and teaching on their wives. Children need the strength of a father's tough and tender love. Both fathers and mothers must commit themselves to caring about the best interests of their children.

The family is God's idea. Our families must be guided by God's standards. Marriage and family counselor H. Norman Wright said, "I believe God's plan and desire is that a family unit include both a man and woman, faithful, healthy, and together for life."[4] Ken B. Canfield, a researcher on the role of fathers, argues that both fathers and mothers are important in the family. The most effective parents have a strong marital relationship characterized by love, trust, and communication. Canfield said that a strong loving bond between husband and wife provides "an atmosphere of security in your home in which your children can grow. You also model what an effective marriage looks like, and thus determine how your children perceive marriage and whether they themselves will eventually be successful when they get married."[5] "The quality of marital life goes a long way toward determining our communication with our children, the sexual protection of our children, our commitment to and satisfaction with our children, and the ability of our children to handle crises."[6]

If love is going to flourish in our homes, husbands must love their wives and wives must love their husbands. This is one of the best gifts parents can give their children. Unreserved commitment to one's mate "unto death do us part" is the cement needed to make a home what God wants it to be.

Learning respect and care for others begins at home. "We love because He first loved us" (1 John 4:19). Many people feel unloved and feel that no one values them. They have difficulty in opening themselves to care deeply for others. Christ demonstrated that God loves us. When we realize that the God who made and controls this universe loves us and considers us of great value in His eyes, then we can know what is most important in life. Everything is different once God is restored to His rightful place.

Knowing that God loves us gives us a new perspective on life. We know we are unworthy and undeserving of God's love, but He loves us anyway. When a believer accepts God's love expressed through Christ's death on the cross, he finds that love makes all things new as God gives new life. In this new life a Christian learns to love others as God has first loved him. "If God so loved us, we also ought to love one another" (1 John 4:11). Love turns sour when bottled up within. God's Spirit helps us learn to express love to God and to others (Romans 5:4; Galatians 5:22).

Jesus said the greatest commandment was "You shall love the Lord your God with all your heart, and with all your soul, and with all your mind and with all your strength" (Mark 12:30). Loving God is more a matter of the will than of the emotions. Some try to manufacture feelings that they suppose means they are loving God. However, we are loving God when we seek to please Him by doing His will. When we love God, pleasing Him becomes the most important thing in life.

Jesus added the second greatest commandment, "You shall love your neighbor as yourself" (Mark 12:31). Christ helps each person have the proper view of himself or herself as a person made in the image of God and of great value to Him. He also teaches us to love and care for others as we care for ourselves. Jesus gave a guideline for loving others, "So whatever you wish that men would do to you, do so to them" (Matthew 7:12).

Someone has said, "Love is the feeling you feel when you feel the feeling you never felt before." This is not what Jesus had in mind. Jesus taught that love acts in the other person's best interests. Regardless of one's feelings, whether friendly or unfriendly, love requires commitment to treat others in the way that is really for their good. Paul said to, "Count others better than yourselves" (Philippians 2:3).

> Love is patient and kind; love is not jealous or boastful; it is not arrogant or rude. Love does not insist on its own way; it is not irritable or resentful; it does not rejoice at wrong, but rejoices in the right. Love bears all things, believes all things, hopes all things, endures all things. Love never ends [Love does not quit loving] (1 Corinthians 13:4-8a).

A businessman was speaking at a Christian conference near the hospital where his father was dying of throat cancer. He did not want to see his father because he resented him for the mistreatment and rejection of many years. The few contacts after his parents divorced left additional scars. His father's cancer had advanced so that he could not speak or hear but had to communicate through written notes.

The son was convinced that, though he did not have warm feelings toward his father, he should still go to visit him. When he arrived he found that his father, facing death's door, had rethought many things. He said he was sorry for mistreating his son and his mother. The son was able to introduce his father to Christ.[7] We must not wait for warm emotions before we show concern for others. We must decide with God's help to act in the other person's best interest. The emotions will follow.

Jesus said, "A new commandment I give to you, that you love one another; even as I have loved you, that you also love one another. By this all men will know that you are my disciples, if you have love for one another" (John 13:34-35). Our Lord not only taught us to love, His life showed us how to love. Through His Spirit Christ enables His followers to love others as He loved.

Hope

Christ not only gives peace and love; He also gives hope to those who trust Him. The joy of life has gone from many faces in our world because they have no hope. They try to cover up their emptiness with drink, drugs, or sexual encounters but they find only more despair. Paul describes them as "having no hope and without God in the world" (Ephesians 2:12). Those who do not believe in God have no basis for hope in this life or in life beyond death.

Herai, a Japanese young man, gave up his Christian faith because of his high school science studies. He renounced God and became a communist. He was involved in the riots that toppled the Kishi government in Kyoto in 1960. One of his friends came to him and asked, "Can Jesus Christ give me any hope in life?"

Herai responded, "Nonsense, there is no God who can give you hope." The young man went home and wrote in his diary and then committed suicide.

The next day, the dead boy's mother called Herai and said, "My son wrote these words in his diary, 'I asked Herai, "Can Jesus Christ give me any hope in life?" and he said, "Nonsense, no God can give you hope."'" This event brought Herai back to his Christian faith. He saw the only hope available is found in Jesus Christ. If there is no God, then we have no hope beyond death. But if God is real, then believers can have hope through Jesus Christ.

Jean-Paul Sartre said he was forlorn because he believed that no God existed. In 1980 he wrote in his journal about despair and hope:

> With this third world war which might break out one day, with this wretched gathering which our planet now is, despair returns to tempt me. The idea that there is no purpose, only petty personal ends for which we fight! We make little revolutions, but there is no goal for mankind. One cannot think such things. They tempt you incessantly, especially if you are old and think "Oh well, I'll be dead in five years at the most." In fact, I think ten, but it might well be five. In any case the world seems ugly, bad, and without hope. There, that's the cry of despair of an old man who will die in despair. But that's exactly what I resist. I know I shall die in hope. But that hope needs a foundation.[8]

Within a month Sartre was dead. What is that foundation that can give us hope in death?

Peter affirmed, "By his great mercy we have been born anew to a living hope through the resurrection of Jesus Christ from the dead, and to an inheritance which is imperishable, undefiled, and unfading, kept in heaven for you" (1 Peter 1:3-4). Paul based our hope of resurrection from the dead on the risen Christ (Philippians 3:10-11; 1 Thessalonians 4:13-18). The Christian hope gives stability as "a sure and steadfast anchor of the soul" (Hebrews 6:19). Paul's prayer is fulfilled in believers, "May the God of hope fill you with all joy and peace in believing, so that by the power of the Holy Spirit you may abound in hope" (Romans 15:13).

A thirteen-year-old boy had a large cancer on his throat. He knew he was going to die. His father, mother, and the preacher were crying at his bedside. The lad comforted them, "It's all right. I'm a Christian."

An older Christian gentleman said, "There are a lot of things in the book of Revelation that I don't understand. But I do know the good guys win!" An important message in the last book in the Bible is that those who are faithful to God unto death can have hope.

Jesus promised us, "Be faithful unto death, and I will give

you the crown of life" (Revelation 2:10). We can have assurance of salvation and a confident hope beyond death if we have accepted Jesus as our Savior and continue faithful to Him unto death. Nothing can take that away from the believer.

CHRISTIANITY STANDS TRUE

1) The New Testament stands true as history.
2) Jesus stands true as the Son of God.
3) The Bible stands true as the Word of God.
4) God stands true in the universe.
5) Christianity stands true in life.

Conclusion

The Story of the Key Flower is an old fairy tale from Great Britain. Mothers liked to tell their children to look for a perfect flower, the Key Flower. If they found the Key Flower and picked it, a fairy would appear, the hillside would open and the person would have access to successive rooms of unlimited treasure.

One day a young man picked a beautiful flower as he walked on a grassy hillside. It was the Key Flower. A fairy appeared. She told him that he could go into successive rooms through an opening in the hillside. He could take all the treasure he wanted but if he ever left a room without the Key Flower all the treasure would turn to dead leaves. "Take all you want but don't forget the best," she cautioned.

The first room had pieces of silver. He gathered all the silver he could carry and brought the flower. The next room contained large pieces of gold. He put down the silver and picked up all the gold he could carry. Before leaving the room he remembered the Key Flower. In the next room he found large, beautiful diamonds. He emptied his pockets of the gold pieces and gathered up all the diamonds he could carry. Thinking of his new found wealth he started into the next room. Too late he remembered, "Take all you want, but don't forget the best." He had forgotten the Key Flower. All the treasure turned to dead leaves.

This story can illustrate this truth. God made each person in His image and provided all the good things of this life. He says, "Take all the good things in this life but don't forget the best." We can be successful in business or in a profession, but if we have not accepted Christ as Savior and been faithful to Him as Lord, all our earthly successes will be as worthless as dead leaves.

Christianity stands true in life. As we surrender our lives to Jesus as Lord, we find the only life worth living. Jesus invites each person as He invited two early disciples, "Come and see" (John 1:39).

Jesus said, "For whoever would save his life will lose it, and whoever loses his life for my sake will find it" (Matthew 16:25). C.S. Lewis explains,

> Give up yourself, and you will find your real self. Lose your life and you will save it. Submit to death, death of your ambitions and favourite wishes every day and death of your whole body in the end: submit with every fibre of your being, and you will find eternal life. Keep back nothing. Nothing that you have not given away will ever be really yours. Nothing in you that has not died will ever be raised from the dead. Look for yourself, and you will find in the long run only hatred, loneliness, despair, rage, ruin, and decay. But look for Christ and you will find Him; and with Him everything else thrown in. [9]

Jesus does not call for blind commitment. He wants an intelligent trust based on the evidence. Convincing answers are available for the big questions. Only in Jesus Christ you can find a solid foundation upon which to build your life. Lighthearted commitment will not do. Christ calls for total submission to His lordship. His challenge remains, "If any man would come after me, let him deny himself and take up his cross and follow me" (Matthew 16:24).

NOTES

Chapter One — The New Testament Stands True as History
Part 1 — Authors and Text

[1]*Tulsa Daily World,* Jan. 5, 1977.

[2]Quotations from early Christian writers are taken from the following sources:

The Ante-Nicene Fathers ed. Alexander Roberts and James Donaldson, Vol. I (Grand Rapids: Wm. B. Eerdmans, 1950); *Nicene and Post-Nicene Fathers* edited by Philip Schaff, First Series, Volume I (Grand Rapids: Wm. B. Eerdmans, 1956); *Nicene and Post-Nicene Fathers* edited by Philip Schaff and Henry Wace, Second Series, Volume I (Grand Rapids: Wm. B. Eerdmans, 1952).

[3]Eusebius, *Ecclesiastical History,* III, 39, 16.

[4]Eusebius, *Ecclesiastical History,* III, 39, 15.

[5]Irenaeus, *Against Heresies,* III, 1, 1.

[6]Eusebius, *Ecclesiastical History,* III, 39, 15.

[7]*Dialog with Trypho the Jew,* chapter 106.

[8]Quoted by V. Taylor, *The Gospel According to St. Mark,* 2nd ed. (New York: St Martin's Press, 1966), p. 3.

[9]Irenaeus, *Against Heresies,* III, 1, 1.

[10]*Dialog with Trypho the Jew,* c., iii.

[11]Quoted in F.F. Bruce, The Acts of the Apostles, 3rd ed. (Grand Rapids, Wm. B. Eerdmans, 1990), p. 1.

[12]Irenaeus, *Against Heresies,* III, 1, 1.

[13]Ibid., III, 10, 1.

[14]Ibid., III, 14, 1.

[15]Quoted in Bettenson, *Documents of the Christian Church* (New York: Oxford University Press, 1963), p. 40.

[16]Irenaeus, *Against Heresies,* III, 1, 1.

[17]Eusebius, *Ecclesiastical History*, VI, xiv, 7.

[18]Paul Barnett, *Is the New Testament Reliable? A Look at the Historical Evidence* (Downers Grove: InterVarsity Press, 1986 [1992]),p. 35.

[19]Quoted in Dewey M. Beegle, *God's Word Into English*, (Grand Rapids: Wm. B. Eerdmans, 1960), pp. 14-15; See also Bruce Metzger, *The Text of the New Testament*, 3rd ed., (New York: Oxford University Press, 1992), pp. 42-45.

[20]Gleason Archer, *A Survey of Old Testament Introduction* rev. ed. (Chicago: Moody Press, 1974), p. 25.

[21]F.F. Bruce *The Books and the Parchments*, rev. ed. (Old Tappan, NJ: Fleming H. Revell Company, 1984), pp. 168, 171.

[22]Stephen Neill and Tom Wright, *The Interpretation of the New Testament*, 1961-1986, 2nd ed. (New York: Oxford University Press, 1988), p. 84.

[23]Paul Barnett, *Is the New Testament Reliable? A Look at the Historical Evidence* (Downers Grove: InterVarsity Press, 1988 [1992]), pp. 46-47.

[24]Ibid.

[25]Quoted in Geisler and Nix, *A General Introduction to the Bible*, rev. ed. (Chicago: Moody Press, 1986), p. 430.

[26]Bruce Metzger, *The Text of the New Testament*, 3rd ed. (New York: Oxford University Press, 1992), p. 8.

[27]B.F. Westcott and F.J.A. Hort, *The New Testament in the Original Greek*, Vol. I (New York: Macmillan, 1881), p. 2.

[28]J.W. McGarvey, *Evidences of Christianity*, (Cincinnati: Standard Publishing Co., 1886), Pt. I, p. 17.

Chapter Two — The New Testament Stands True as History
Part 2 — Historical Accuracy

[1]Earle E. Cairns, "Christian Faith and History," in *Christianity and the World of Thought*, edited by Hudson Armerding (Chicago: Moody Press, 1968), p. 152.

[2]Kenneth Kantzer, "Can I Really Trust the Bible?" in *Tough Questions Christians Ask*, edited by David Neff (Wheaton: Victor Books, 1989), pp. 117-118.

[3]William Ramsey, *The Bearing of Recent Discoveries on the Trustworthiness of the New Testament* (Grand Rapids: Baker Book House, 1911), pp. 22, 79. See William Ramsey, *St. Paul the Traveler and the Roman Citizen*, 14th ed. (London: Hodder and Stoughton, 1920), pp. 7-8.

[4]F.F. Bruce, *Jesus and Christian Origins Outside the New Testament* (Grand Rapids: Wm. B. Eerdmans, 1974), p. 201.

[5]F.F. Bruce, "The Confirmation of the New Testament," in *Revelation and the Bible*, edited by Carl F.H. Henry (Grand Rapids: Baker Book House, 1969), p. 332.

[6]Nelson Glueck, *Rivers in the Desert* (New York: Farrar, Strauss, Cudahy, 1959), p. 31.

[7]*Antiquities*, XX, 200. See R.T. France, *The Evidence for Jesus* (Downers Grove: InterVarsity Press, 1986), pp. 25-32 and F.F. Bruce, *Jesus and Christian Origins Outside the New Testament* (Grand Rapids: Wm. B. Eerdmans, 1974), pp. 40-41.

[8]Quoted by J. Klasner, *Jesus of Nazareth* (New York: Macmillin, 1929), p. 34.

[9]*The Babylonian Talmud* (London: The Soncino Press, 1969), Sanhedrin, 43a.

[10]Tacitus, *Annals*, xv, 44.

[11]Pliny of Bithynia, *Epistles*, x. 96.

[12]I am indebted to Dr. Lewis Foster for this illustration from Alexander the Great.

Chapter Three — Jesus Stands True as the Son of God
Part 1 — Claims to Deity

[1]C.S. Lewis, *Mere Christianity*, rev. ed. (New York: Macmillan, 1952), p. 56.

Chapter Four — Jesus Stands True as the Son of God
Part 2 — Credentials of Deity

[1]Gilbert West, *Observations on the History and Events of the Resurrection of Jesus Christ*. George Lyttleton, *The Conversion of St. Paul* (New York: American Tract Society, n.d.).

[2]Merrill C. Tenney, *The Reality of the Resurrection* (Chicago: Moody Press, 1963), pp. 116-120.

[3]A.B. Bruce, *The Training of the Twelve* (New York: Harper and Brothers, n.d.), p. 495.

[4]Speech before the National Religious Broadcasters Convention, February, 1984.

[5]Justin Martyr, *Second Apology*.

[6]Michael Green, *Running From Reality* (Downers Grove: InterVarsity Press, 1983), p. 64.

[7]Ibid.

Chapter Five — The Bible Stands True as the Word of God
Part 1 — Inspiration Claimed

[1]Plato, *Phaedo*, 85C.

[2]Kenneth Kantzer, "Christ and Scripture," *HIS*, (June, 1982), 18.

[3]Josephus, *Against Apion*, I, 7.

[4]Clement of Rome, *First Epistle of Clement*, XLV.

[5]Justin Martyr, *Apology*, I, 36.

[6]Justin Martyr, *Dialog With Trypho*, LXV.

[7]Irenaeus, *Against Heresies*, ii, 28, 2.

[8]Augustine, *Letter*, 82, i, 3.

[9]Thomas Aquinas, *Summa Theologica*, I, A1, a, 10.

[10]Martin Luther, *Works*, IX, p. 1481.

[11]Martin Luther, *Works*, XIX, p. 1073.

[12]John Calvin, *Commentaries on the Pastoral Epistles* (Grand Rapids: Wm. B. Eerdmans, 1949), 2 Timothy 3:16.

[13]John Calvin, *Commentaries on the Epistle to the Hebrews* (Grand Rapids: Wm. B. Eerdmans, 1949), Epistle Dedicatory, p. xxi.

Chapter Six — The Bible Stands True as the Word of God
Part 2 — Inspiration Confirmed

[1]R.T. France, "Jesus Christ and the Bible," in *Eerdman's Handbook to the Bible*, edited by David and Pat Alexander (Grand Rapids: Wm. B. Eerdmans, 1973), p. 40.

²James I. Packer, *God Has Spoken*, (Grand Rapids: Baker Book House, 1979), p. 119.

³Clement of Rome, *First Epistle of Clement*, 47.

⁴Ibid., p. 45.

⁵Justin Martyr, *Apology*, I, 119.

⁶Irenaeus, *Against Heresies*, III, 1, 1.

⁷Ibid., II, 28, 2.

⁸Kenneth Kantzer, "Christ and Scripture," *HIS* (June, 1982), 17.

⁹William Barclay, *The Gospel of Matthew*, rev. ed., Vol, I, (Philadelphia: Westminster Press, 1975), p. 292.

Chapter Seven — God Stands True in the Universe
Part 1 — Design in the Physical
Universe and in the Human Body

¹George O. Asbell, "Exploring the Farthest Reaches of Space," *National Geographic* (May, 1969), p. 629.

²Quoted in *God Exists*, filmstrip series published by Our Sunday Visitor, Inc., Huntington, Indiana.

³Ibid.

⁴W.M. Smart, *The Origin of the Earth* (New York: Cambridge University Press, 1951), p. 235.

⁵Robert Jastrow, *God and the Astronomers* (New York: W. W. Norton, 1978), p. 111.

⁶Vaden Miles, Everett Phelps, Ray Sherwood, Willard Parsons, *College Physical Science* (New York: Harper and Row, 1964), p. 365.

⁷Robert Gange, *Origins and Destiny* (Waco, TX: Word Books, 1986), p. 59.

⁸John Whitcomb and Donald DeYoung, *The Moon: Its Creation, Form, and Significance* (Winona Lake: BMH Books, 1978), pp. 130-131.

⁹Leonard Engel and the editors of Life, *The Sea* (New York: Time, Inc., 1961), p. 10.

¹⁰Whittaker Chambers, *The Witness* (New York: Random House, 1952), pp. 16-17.

[11]Paul Brand and Phillip Yancey, *Fearfully and Wonderfully Made* (Grand Rapids: Zondervan Publishing House, 1980), p. 70.
[12]Ibid., pp. 45-46.
[13]Robert Gange, *Origins and Destiny* (Waco, TX: Word Books, 1986), p. 72.
[14]Ibid., p. 76.
[15]Ibid., p. 71.

**Chapter Eight — God Stands True in the Universe
Part 2 — Design in the
Plant and Animal World**

[1]K. H. Luling, "The Archer Fish," *Scientific American*, (July, 1963).
[2]Dr. Ed Blick, lecture at Ozark Christian College, Joplin, Missouri, September 5, 1979.
[3]Charles Darwin, *The Origin of Species*, first ed. reprint (New York: Avenel Books, 1979 of 1859 edition), p. 217.
[4]Charles Darwin in a letter to Asa Gray, April 3, 1860. Cited in Norman Macbeth, *Darwin Retried: An Appeal to Reason* (Boston: Gambit: 1971), p. 101.
[5]Charles Darwin, *Life and Letters*, Vol. I, 282. Cited by Robert T. Clark and James D. Bales, *Why Scientists Accept Evolution* (Grand Rapids: Baker Book House, 1966), p. 38.
[6]Ibid., p. 285, quoted in the above source.
[7]Julian Huxley, *Evolution In Action* (New York: Harper and Brothers, 1953), pp. 41-42.
[8]Paul S. Moorhead and Martin M. Kaplan, *Mathematical Challenges to the Neo-Darwinian Interpretation of Evolution* (Philadelphia: Wistar Institute Press, 1967).
[9]Fred Hoyle and Chandra Wickramasinghe, *Evolution from Space* (London: Dent, 1981), pp. 24-26.
[10]Chandra Wickramasinghe, "Science and the Divine Origin of Life," in *The Intellectuals Speak Out About God* edited by Roy Abraham Varghese (Dallas: Lewis and Stanley, 1984), pp. 23-37, also viii.

Chapter Nine — Christianity Stands True in Life
Part 1 — Meaning and Freedom

[1]Arthur Blessit, *Life's Greatest Trip*, p. 11.
[2]Frederick Nietzsche, *The Gay Science* [125], quoted by Walter Kaufmann in *The Portable Nietzsche* (New York: The Viking Press, 1954), p. 95.
[3]Ibid.
[4]Jean-Paul Sartre, *Existentialism and Human Emotions* (New York: Philosophical Library, 1957), p. 22.
[5]Sigmund Freud, *Civilization and Its Discontents* (New York: W. W. Norton and Co., 1962), p. 23.
[6]Quoted in H.R. Rookmaaker, *Modern Art and the Death of a Culture* (Downers Grove: InterVarsity Press, 1970), p. 174.
[7]Blaise Pascal, *Thoughts: An Apology for Christianity* (Cleveland: World Publishing Company, 1955), p. 234.
[8]Augustine, *Confessions*, I, 1, 1.
[9]Quoted by Charles Colson, *Against the Night* (Ann Arbor: Servant Books, 1989), p. 93.
[10]Aldous Huxley, *Ends and Means*, pp. 270f. Quoted in Michael Green, *Running From Reality* (Downers Grove: InterVarsity Press, 1983), p. 82.

Chapter Ten — Christianity Stands True in Life
Part 2 — Peace, Love, Hope

[1]Aleksandr Solzhenitsyn, "Men Have Forgotten God," *National Review* (July 22, 1983), p. 872.
[2]Bertrand Russell, *The Impact of Science on Society* (Winchester: Allen and Unwin, Inc., 1953), p. 59.
[3]Ashley Montagu, "The Awesome Power of Human Love" *Reader's Digest* (February, 1963), pp. 80-81. This article is a condensation of his book, *The Humanization of Man*.
[4]H. Norman Wright, *The Family Is Still a Great Idea* (Ann Arbor: Servant Publications, 1992), pp. 14-15.
[5]Ken B. Canfield, *The 7 Secrets of Effective Fathers* (Wheaton, IL: Tyndale House Publishers, 1992), pp. 120-121.
[6]Ibid., p. 122.

[7]Keith Miller, *A Second Touch* (Waco, TX: Word Books, 1967), pp. 89-91.

[8]Quoted by Michael Green, *The Day Death Died* (Downers Grove: InterVarsity, 1982), p. 103.

[9]C.S. Lewis, *Mere Christianity*, rev. ed. (New York: Macmillan, 1952), p. 190.

SUGGESTED READING

GENERAL

Boyd, Gregory A. and Edward K. Boyd. *Letters from a Skeptic: A Son Wrestles with His Father's Questions About Christianity*. Wheaton: Victor Books, 1994.

Casteel, Herbert. *Beyond a Reasonable Doubt*. Joplin: College Press, 1990.

Cottrell, Jack. *His Truth*. Joplin: College Press, 1989.

Craig, William Lane. *Reasonable Faith: Christian Truth and Apologetics*. Wheaton: Crossway Books, 1994.

Geisler, Norman and Ronald Brooks. *When Skeptics Ask*. Wheaton, IL: Victor Books, 1990.

Hoover, Arlie J. *Dear Agnos: Letters to An Agnostic In Defense of Christianity*. Joplin, College Press, 1992.

Lewis, C.S. *Mere Christianity*. New York: Macmillan, 1952.

Little, Paul. *Know Why You Believe*, 3rd ed. Downers Grove: InterVarsity, 1988.

McDowell, Josh. *Evidence That Demands a Verdict*, rev. ed. San Bernardino: Here's Life, 1979.

McGrath, Alister E. *Explaining Your Faith*. Grand Rapids: Zondervan, 1989.

CHRISTIANITY STANDS TRUE

——————— . *Intellectuals Don't Need God and Other Modern Myths: Building Bridges to Faith Through Apologetics.* Grand Rapids: Zondervan, 1993.

Miethe, Terry L. and Gary R. Habermas, *Why Believe? God Exists!* Joplin: College Press, 1993.

Miethe, Terry L. *Living Your Faith: Closing the Gap Between Mind and Heart.* Joplin: College Press, 1993.

Shelly, Rubel. *Prepare to Answer: A Defense of the Christian Faith.* Grand Rapids: Baker, 1990.

Sire, James. *Why Should Anyone Believe Anything at All?* Downers Grove: InterVarsity, 1994.

——————— . *Chris Christman Goes to College and Faces the Challenge of Relativism, Individualism and Pluralism.* Downers Grove: InterVarsity, 1993.

THE NEW TESTAMENT STANDS TRUE AS HISTORY

Anderson, J.N.D. *Jesus Christ: The Witness of History.* Downers Grove: InterVarsity, 1985.

Barnett, Paul. *Is the New Testament Reliable? A Look at the Historical Evidence.* Downers Grove: InterVarsity, 1986, 1992.

Bruce, F.F. *The New Testament Documents: Are They Reliable?* 5th rev. ed. Downers Grove: InterVarsity, 1960.

——————— . *Jesus and Christian Origins Outside the New Testament.* Grand Rapids: Eerdmans, 1974.

France, R.T. *Evidence for Jesus.* Downers Grove: InterVarsity, 1986.

Greenlee, J. Harold. *Introduction to New Testament Textual Criticism.* Revised. Peabody, MA: Hendrickson, 1995.

Lightfoot, Neil. *How We Got the Bible*, rev. ed. Abilene, TX: ACU Press, 1986.

McDowell, Josh and Bill Wilson. *He Walked Among Us: Evidence for the Historical Jesus.* San Bernardino: Here's Life, 1988.

Montgomery, John Warwick. *History and Christianity.* Downers Grove: InterVarsity, 1964.

JESUS STANDS TRUE AS THE SON OF GOD

Buell, Jon A. and O. Quentin Hyder. *Jesus: God, Ghost or Guru?* Grand Rapids: Zondervan, 1978.

Green, Michael. *The Day Death Died.* Downers Grove: Inter-Varsity, 1991.

_____ . *The Empty Cross of Jesus.* Downers Grove: InterVarsity, 1984.

Habermas, Gary and Antony Flew. *Did Jesus Rise from the Dead? The Resurrection Debate.* New York: Harper & Row, 1987.

Little, Paul E. "Jesus Christ" in *Know What You Believe*, rev. ed. Wheaton: Victor Books, 1987.

McDonald, H.D. *Jesus: Human and Divine.* Grand Rapids: Zondervan, 1968.

McDowell, Josh. *More Than a Carpenter.* Wheaton: Tyndale, 1980.

_____ . *Jesus: A Biblical Defense of His Deity.* San Bernardino: Here's Life, 1983.

McGrath, Alister E. *Understanding Jesus.* Grand Rapids: Zondervan, 1987.

Morris, Leon. *The Lord From Heaven*. Grand Rapids: Eerdmans, 1958.

Pressley, Johnny. "Jesus Christ," in *Essentials of Christian Faith*, ed. by Steve Burris, pages 49-68. Joplin: College Press, 1992.

Stott, John. *The Authentic Jesus*. Downers Grove: InterVarsity, 1985.

——————— . *Basic Christianity*, 2nd ed., pages 11-60. Grand Rapids: Eerdmans, 1971.

THE BIBLE STANDS TRUE AS THE WORD OF GOD

Bruce, F.F. *The Canon of Scripture*. Downers Grove: InterVarsity, 1988.

Cottrell, Jack. *Solid: The Authority of the Bible*. Joplin: College Press, 1991.

Geisler, Norman, ed. *Inerrancy*. Grand Rapids: Zondervan, 1979.

Henry, Carl F.H., ed. *Revelation and the Bible*. Grand Rapids: Baker, 1958.

Morris, Leon. *I Believe in Revelation*. Grand Rapids: Eerdmans, 1976.

Stott, John. *You Can Trust the Bible*. Grand Rapids: Discovery House, 1991.

Wenham, John. *Christ and the Bible*, 3rd rev. ed. Grand Rapids: Baker, 1994.

——————— . *Christ and the Bible*, 3rd ed. Grand Rapids: Baker, 1994.

GOD STANDS TRUE IN THE UNIVERSE

Brand, Paul and Philip Yancey. *Fearfully and Wonderfully Made*. Grand Rapids: Zondervan, 1980.

_____ . *In His Image*. Grand Rapids: Zondervan, 1984.

_____ . *Pain: The Gift that Nobody Wants*. New York: HarperCollins, 1993.

Cosgrove, Mark D. *The Amazing Body Human: God's Design for Personhood*. Grand Rapids: Baker, 1987.

Davis, Percival. *Of Pandas and People*. Dallas: Haughton Publishing Company, 1989.

Denton, Michael. *Evolution: A Theory in Crisis*. Bethesda, MD: Adler and Adler, 1986.

Gange, Robert. *Origins and Destiny: A Scientist Examines God's Handiwork*. Waco, TX: Word Books, 1986.

Gish, Duane T. *Creation Scientists Answer Their Critics*. El Cajon, CA: Institute for Creation Research, 1993.

Lubenow, Marvin L. *Bones of Contention: A Creationist Assesssment of Human Fossils*. Grand Rapids: Baker, 1992.

Pearcey, Nancy R. and Charles B. Thaxton. *The Soul of Science: Christian Faith and Natural Philosophy*. Wheaton: Crossway, 1994.

Taylor, Paul S. *The Illustrated Origins Answer Book*, 3rd ed. Mesa: Eden Productions, 1991.

CHRISTIANITY STANDS TRUE IN LIFE

Breese, Dave. *Seven Men Who Rule the World from the Grave.* Chicago: Moody, 1990.

Colson, Charles. *Against the Night.* Ann Arbor: Servant, 1989.

Crossley, Robert. *We Want to Live.* Downers Grove: Inter-Varsity, 1967.

Green, Michael. *New Life, New Lifestyle.* Downers Grove: Inter-Varsity, 1973.

——————. *Running from Reality.* Downers Grove: Inter-Varsity, 1983.

Morris, Thomas V. *Making Sense of It All.* Grand Rapids: Eerdmans, 1992.

Veith, Gene Edward, Jr. *Postmodern Times: A Christian Guide to Contemporary Thought and Culture.* Wheaton: Crossway, 1994.

ABOUT THE AUTHOR

Lynn Gardner

Academic Dean (1981 to present) and
  Professor of Apologetics (1973 to present)
  at Ozark Christian College, Joplin, Missouri

Formerly Professor (1967-1973) and
  Academic Dean (1972-1973) at Central Christian
  College, Moberly, Missouri

Served two years as Associate Editor, College Press,
  Joplin, Missouri

Held preaching ministries in Missouri, Kansas,
  and California.

Education:
    B. Th., Ozark Christian College, 1961
    B. A., California State College, Stanislaus, 1965
    M. A., Wheaton Graduate School, 1967
    Ed. D., University of Arkansas, 1991

Writings:
Contributor to religious periodicals.
Author of *Twenty-Six Lessons on Luke, Part I* (College Press, 1990) and *Ozark Christian College: A Vision of Teaching the Word of Christ in the Spirit of Christ* (Ozark Christian College, 1992).
Co-author of *Learning from God's Word* (College Press, 1989).
Editor of *The Mind of Christ: A Tribute to Seth Wilson* (College Press, 1987).